THINGS

THINGS

Four Metabletic Reflections

by

J. H. van den Berg,

Ph.D., M.D.,

Professor at the University of Leiden

DUQUESNE UNIVERSITY PRESS, PITTSBURGH, PA.

Editions E. Nauwelaerts, Louvain

First Printing

Library of Congress catalog card number: 74-125033

The Duquesne University Press
Pittsburgh, Pa. 15219

Printed in the United States of America

iv

CONTENTS

PREFACE

The first translation of this work was made by Dr. M. Jacobs, who for many years has closely followed Dr. van den Berg's thinking. His translation was carefully revised by the undersigned. Our thanks is due to Miss Edith O'Loughlin for her attempts to improve the readability of this work. Her literary efforts, however, often met our recalcitrant opposition; hence she shouldn't be blamed for any literary deficiencies that may still be found in it.

Henry J. Koren

DIMENSIONS

For the past fifteen minutes I have been sitting on the front porch of my friend's country-house. Before me lies the garden with a lawn bordered by flowers and shrubs. Beyond the shrubs, the woods begin. On the left is a meadow and in the distance a grove of trees. Between me and the garden there is the balustrade of a porch. A few wooden steps lead down to the garden, which lies somewhat lower than the porch on which I am seated. I have been here now for exactly two weeks, a guest of my friend. He wanted to remodel the house and asked me to help him.

This is the kind of vacation I like because we worked hard on the house, which looks much better now. We are now busy with the porch, which runs the full length of the house, and this very length worries my friend. It is very easy, he says, to spoil the facade and he is right. This wooden addition determines the entire look of the house. We have finished with the floor, replacing it with white pine boards that still smell. I am seated in the midst of their fragrance.

It is summer. The sun has reached the porch; it shines on a part of the new floor and broils the wood there. The heat is oppressive; I can feel it coming from all directions. Now that the sun shines on the small roof of the porch, I can even feel the heat coming from above. Yet, I am still in the shade. What a summer! Two weeks without a drop of rain.

Later today we will continue our work on the balustrade. The old balusters were rotten and we have cut them out. The new ones which are ready can simply be fastened with screws to the upper and lower rails. Some of them are already in their place. Their shape is different from the old ones. The latter were of the same width over their entire length and oval-shaped across; the new ones are angular-shaped across and tapering toward the top. Their tapered shape makes the house look wider and therefore less high.

With the old balusters the house looked too high; my friend was right in this. We discussed the matter at length and even studied the effect by first using cardboard balusters. When we put these in place upside down, with the tapered ends at the bottom, the vertical dimensions of the house looked entirely out of proportion. But now it will be much more of a summer-house than it used to be, a true country-house in harmony with the green scenery around it. We must still discuss whether we will paint the balusters or simply varnish the wood which is excellent in quality. One baluster, which is lying on the table, cannot be used because it is too short. It measures only one meter, ten centimeters less than the others. One meter and ten centimeters may seem a lot, but it isn't that much if one considers that the balusters will be sunk into the bottom rail. The balustrade itself is only eighty centimeters high.

I take the short baluster from the table, which stands fully in the sun. The wood is warm through and through. It is high noon and the air is perfectly still. Everything simmers in the heat — the lawn, the flowers and the trees. My friend has gone for a nap, so I am all by myself, alone. I could not do that; it would leave me too sleepy all day. But I like to sit alone for a while and meditate a little in the peace and quiet of this summer afternoon. I am not entirely alone though, because the dog is lying in a corner of the porch which the sun has not yet reached. He is a long-haired, black animal, which keeps jumping around us. Now he is sleeping, with his hindlegs stretched out, so as to catch a maximum of coolness from the floor and to have the least possible trouble from his own body heat.

The animal is motionless. Will he be able to resist the temptation of the baluster if I throw it? I raise it and call the dog. He jerks up his head, sees the piece of wood and knows what I mean. His tail moves gently to and fro between his legs. Shouting my customary "Get it!", I throw the baluster on the lawn, right up to the flowers. The wood's flat surface reflects the sunlight. The dog sees the wood fall down; he raises his head a little higher, but does not get up. His tail stops wagging; he puts his head on his left paw, gives me another look, and then goes back to sleep. It is too hot and oppressive, to run around. Everything is quiet and motionless around me, except for a few small cumulus clouds which I can vaguely see moving above the meadow in the distance. There is motion over there.

The reflection of the sun on the wood still strikes my eyes. I should not have thrown that piece of wood. It was not right to have shouted and thrown things at this quiet hour. Now the short, smooth baluster lies there, close to the flowers. That isn't right either. It could be lying here on the table without any objections, between screws, screwdrivers, a plane and some shavings. Later I will remove that baluster from the lawn. **It is** too short, we said, but over there it no longer looks too short.

Is it only one meter long? That's hard to believe; it clearly seems to be longer. Its location and the things over there must account for that, just as the height of this house depends more or less, on the elegance of the balustrade. The height itself remains the same, as does that of the piece of wood, whether it lies here or there. But looking at the baluster, I have trouble believing that. It clearly looks longer than one meter. I would say, one meter and twenty or twenty-five centimeters. I am reasonably good at estimating length. Am I mistaken, then? I must be mistaken; there can be no doubt about it. But every time I look at the baluster, my doubt is reborn. That piece of wood no longer than one meter? If I am to believe this, my eyes are then deceiving me. But on what can I base my belief then? What is the argument which takes away my doubt and gives me the right — really justifies me — to believe that that piece of wood on the grass there is one meter, no more and no less? This brings us up to our first meditation.

First Reflection

At first it does not seem difficult to maintain the conviction that the baluster on the grass is just as long as the baluster here on the table. I pick up the tape measure with which I measured the piece of wood when it was still here in front of me. The tape has a mark indicating 100 centimeters. So I could tell myself: go out into the garden and measure the baluster out there with the same tape. I would then find again 100 centimeters; hence the baluster is just as long there as it is here. My eyes bear witness to it. But what is the value of my seeing? When I looked at the piece of wood from the porch, a few minutes ago. I rejected the reliability of my eye; am I now invited to trust that same eye? When I first compared the baluster out there with one here, I was sitting on the porch. Then I left the porch so that I could measure the baluster with the same tape I had used before on the porch. But can this consideration really help me? I say, "the same tape," but is this really true? Just as true, it seems to me, as the statement, "the same baluster" which was exactly the statement that gave rise to my doubt.

What do I really want when I say: go out into the garden and measure? It implies at least that I get up, accept the heat of the sun, cross the lawn, bend down in the sun at the border, put the tape beside the baluster, and read a number. But all this is too much now in this heat; I am not going to do it. Thus I desire something which I will not do. This difficulty, however, does not seem important. I certainly could do the things I have just enumerated; I could walk out into the garden and measure that piece of wood. Disregarding the fact which should not be simply neglected that I then do something to which I somehow have to force myself, I fulfill the condition that needs to be fulfilled if I am to measure the thing: I get up, move over the lawn, bend down by the border, take out the tape and put it alongside the baluster. If I do not fulfill this condition, I cannot measure and, consequently, I lack the simple proof of comparative measurement that the baluster here is just as long as the baluster there.

But are such ideas not far-fetched and sterile? I don't know. What is meant by the term "condition" in the happenings mentioned above? Are they circumstances having nothing to do with the measuring as such? Or are they genuine conditions, without which comparative measurement is not possible and without which the result of this measurement must be doubted? What am I to think of the two lengths if the second supposition remains obscure? But, on the other hand, what I see is not obscure: the two lengths are unequal. Thus my doubt remains. Is there perhaps a method of measuring and comparing which will permit me to remain seated where I am?

It is not difficult to discover such a method. For example, buy two identical tapes, keep one and give the other to an assistant and then ask him to stand in the garden with his tape. After rechecking the length of the baluster with my new tape to make sure that it is indeed 100 centimeters, I then throw the baluster to him. He takes his own measuring tape and calls: "One hundred centimeters." One hundred here, one hundred there; the proof has been delivered; the baluster there and the baluster here are equal in length.

The proof? Again, conditions must be fullfilled, perhaps even more conditions than in the first method. For there are many differences between me and my assistant which I neglect in my second approach without knowing what they mean for my proof. He is there, I am here. He is outside in the garden, I am sheltered by the porch. He is exposed to the direct heat of the sun, I am seated in the shade. Moreover, he knows nothing about the house and our worries about it; I know the house as well as the garden in which he stands. I know what my friend wishes to do with it. I know my friend, that he is resting and that everything here is quiet. In short, I am conscious of the fact that this is a summer afternoon in this spot where I am seated and from which I threw the baluster. He knows nothing, or hardly anything, of all this. He is only an assistant, a "neutral" man in a "neutral" place.

Why, then, should his measurements be the same as mine?

There are so many differences between us, and I don't know what influence any of these has on the act of measuring. Thus I don't have the right to assume that such an influence does not exist. If I am prudent, then I conclude that the dimensions are equal only if I neglect all those differences, that is, only if I meet all conditions implied in the negation that those differences are important. Only then is our measuring equal.

Our measuring would be unconditionally equal if we were together in the carpenter shop, both with the same tape and the baluster in front of us. But in that case the difference between the baluster there and the baluster here would be eliminated; yet it is precisely this difference that I wish to know. Therefore the action of my assistant cannot be accepted as a valid approach to ascertain this difference or to discover whether there is none.

Very little is changed in this respect if I substitute my friend for the assistant and assume that my friend is first with me on the porch and then at my request goes out on the lawn to measure the baluster. My friend knows about the house, the lawn, the balusters and what we intend to do with them. He saw, let me assume, that the baluster first was lying on the table. He also saw me throw it and he and I both looked at that piece of wood — now so long — out there on the grass. To this extent my friend and I are equal; while reading his tape out there on the lawn there is a chance that he will not be completely immune to the impression of the "long" baluster he saw from the porch.

Perhaps he will shout: "What do you know! One meter long." Or, "One meter of course!" He could even say, "An optical illusion." However, my neutral assistant would not have been able to make any of those exclamations because he didn't know anything about the baluster. But even if my friend and I are in complete harmony with respect to our knowing, seeing and judging, it still remains true that he measures out there on the lawn and not here on the porch where I see the baluster. He is in the garden, and I am seated on the porch. And what this difference means, I still don't know. Therefore, I still don't have the right to assume that this difference is irrelevant. My doubt persists.

Other suppositions also can be made for the same purpose of determining whether the baluster there is equal in length to the baluster here. But even before I can formulate them in detail, it becomes obvious that one by one they will fail. One of these suppositions, however, interests me, not because it could offer an advantage over the others for the measurement of the baluster, but because it contains some particulars that deserve reflection. It is the following.

I mark the baluster on the table with lines, at intervals of one centimeter, so that the baluster itself becomes a measuring rod. I then throw it out on the lawn, assuming that it will land exactly in the same place and in the same position as before. I then take my binoculars and look at it. The measuring lines are all visible, so that I myself can now read that the baluster is 10, 30 and 100 centimeters long. Does this justify me now to conclude that the baluster here is just as long as it is out there?

Not at all, so it seems to me. The objections are so obvious that they need not even be enumerated. The main difficulty is that I do not know what happens when the baluster is thrown. What do I do when I change the position of an object? What influence does change of place have on dimensions? I really don't know. Then, for the same reason as before, I cannot assume that the dimension which I read with my binoculars is the same which I marked before I threw the piece of wood.

There is another serious difficulty in the assumption of using binoculars and pre-marking the wood with measuring lines. When I use the binoculars to see the lines, I literally magnify the baluster in order to be able to observe its length. A very strange procedure, to say the least. May I, in order to determine the size of an object, magnify it? One can justifiably ask whether in that case I do not irrevocably displace that dimension. I find an enlargement of a dimension which I do not know; and what could I possibly do with that?

What do binoculars do to the observed object? The answer is not easy. To hold fast to concrete experience, let us repeat the question with respect to the garden here, to which, in my thought experiment, I direct the binoculars. Before using them, I once more survey my surroundings: a garden with a lawn, a border of flowers, trees, a sky above, a summerlike complex, and within it, somewhat incongrously, the baluster. An harmonious whole, with a piece of wood that doesn't fit; and this is perhaps one reason why it is so large, excessively large.

Now I pick up the binoculars and focus my eyes, my "armed" eyes, on the baluster. The totality — the garden in the summer — has disappeared. My binoculars cannot encompass the garden; even the lawn alone is too large for that. I see a section of it, only a small section with the baluster on it. True, I do not doubt that what I see now is connected with what I first saw without the binoculars. But neither can I doubt that what I see with my binoculars is different. It is a simmering, spherically limited, small piece of more or less meaningless grass, on which lies a slightly unfamiliar piece of wood with markings.

With the naked eye I could still ask whether the baluster there is "still" or "of course" is just as long as the baluster here, but that doubt becomes meaningless now that I look through the binoculars. How long is that piece of wood in my perfect lens? I have no idea; I don't even have any point of comparison. For the grass around the baluster has equally indefinable dimensions in my binoculars. Is the grass long? Or short? The questions lose their meaning here. The binoculars change everything and play havoc with the concept of dimension. The binoculars, I am told, magnify ten times, exactly ten times, but it could just as well be twenty or thirty times. These numbers are meaningless when I look at the baluster through my binoculars. I have to be told about their power of enlargement, but even then the information that it is ten, twenty, or thirty remains fruitless. I have to accept it, but without the binoculars, I don't have to accept anything. Things are as they are; they have their own dimension. And if they didn't what could *dimension* then possibly be?

To enlarge is to see outside the dimension which the things have, no matter how variable that dimension may be. In front of me stands the table, a thing with a size of its own. On this table lie various objects — chisels, screws, a plane and an ash tray — each one a thing with a size of its own. If I carry the table with the objects outside and look at all these things again from my porch, the changed size is related to the one I saw first, and it remains the things' own size, regardless of how that size changes. I cannot fail to observe this. The baluster is longer but remains the same in that it retains its own — albeit variable — dimension. Now, this dimension is lost when I use my binoculars, for the baluster loses its dimension, along with its own character. This, too, can be seen. The baluster which I see through the binoculars possesses an unreal character.

This difference is just as evident when I look at the baluster through a simple magnifying glass. I then see details which I would never have been able to see with the naked eye, for the simple reason that the magnifying glass permits me to go beyond the boundaries of the naked eye. But this means that the magnifying glass forces the wood over the boundaries of its ordinary dimensions. This crossing of boundaries is even more evident if I use a microscope. I can make a slide of the wood, so thin that light shines through it, so that I can observe the structure of the wood under the microscope.

The structure of the wood? That's a premature statement. In reality, I see the structure of the enlarged wood, and I don't yet know what this really means. Undoubtedly, what I see is related to the wood as I know it — the short history of making the slide tells me this — but how this relationship should be interpreted remains obscure. Is what I see still wood? The ordinary aspect of wood, at any rate, has disappeared. I see a network of cells, a finely formed, artistic network, belonging to a tree, a tree that is five kilometers long.

Five kilometers? Why? I assume here that my microscope is set for a magnification of 500 and that the tree from which the slice was taken was ten meters in height. I have never seen a tree five kilometers tall and, undoubtedly, I will never see one. This must be relevant with respect to the nature of what I see through the microscope. I wish to see and know my tree, my baluster, my object with its dimensions, its own determined dimensions. But this is not with any and all dimensions, as I see when I observe the wood under my microscope and don't worry about what magnification is. A tree either has one dimension — its own — or any dimensions, and that is no dimension at all. My belief in the tree that was five kilometers high is not very great; I believe in the tree that stood ten meters high, five or six times my own length. This is its dimensions, its length, strictly its own size.

Nevertheless, I wouldn't do justice to the reality of the microscope if I left matters at that. Let us therefore return to the question: What do I see when I see cells? If I continue to be prudent — and what else should I be? — I observe that I see wood which, by magnification beyond its limits, exhibits cells. The magnification is the condition, for only if I magnify do I see the cells; only if I do not respect the dimension of the wood itself do I observe cells. Must we say, then, that there are no cells if the wood isn't magnified?

This question deserves a well-considered answer. The unmagnified wood has a structure which I can feel with my fingernails. I can drive my knife into the wood to learn more about this structure. When my friend and I were busy with sawing and planing the balusters, we learned to know this structure in still another way. Pinewood is pinewood, no matter how we shape or refinish it. The structure of the wood which I see and feel is the bearer of all properties. Nothing was or is lacking in it; that is, in this structure there is no need for cells. Cells would even be out of place in this visible and tangible structure. What would be the use of cells if the wood as such is the bearer of all its properties and responds to all the operations which we perform on it?

This consideration, however, need not lead to the conviction that there are no cells. They exist, provided I use the microscope. When I use this instrument, it reveals a new structure, of a different nature. And special attention is drawn to the fact that this new structure also is complete and the bearer of all the properties implied in the new reality given by this structure. Nothing, again, is lacking in this structure, as the science concerned with it has proved abundantly.

It is true, of course, that in many respects this structure needs to be further clarified. However, one could really doubt whether everything pertaining to it will ever be fully clarified. Nevertheless, no man of research doubts the fact that the structure revealed by the microscope is complete, that is meaningfully self-consistent. This structure also is self-sufficient: the slide under the microscope doesn't need the tree; the latter would even be out of place with respect to the slide.

In this way two realities can be distinguished, both of which are self-consistent and self-sufficient and, nonetheless, related to each other. The relationship of these two systems deserves special attention. It may be illustrated as follows.

I cut a branch from the tree, make a slide for my microscope and discover deviations in the cells, which a specialist identifies as mycosis. Under his guidance I can also see the fungal hyphae in the slide. In principle, it is then possible for me to go back to the tree from which the slide came and to treat this sorry-looking tree in the light of my microscopic findings and with the advice of an expert. The wood as such will then be improved, the tree will become healthy. The two structures are so intimately related that such a procedure is possible.

But it would be premature on my part to conclude that in such a procedure I remain within one and the same structure. By the way of the "second" structure — the magnified slide — I can reach the "first," that of the tree as such. It would be as though I would use a necessary detour to reach that purpose, as though I would travel to my destination by way of a foreign country. The trip offers numerous advantages, but at the same time the danger that existing boundaries will be disregarded. One could easily be busy with the second structure while erroneously thinking that one is learning details about the first.

All this becomes perhaps most evident if one uses the microscope for one's own body and discovers there, in the second structure of that body, certain peculiarities, let us say again, an illness. To be more specific, I make a microscopic blood slide of my body, look at the slide through the microscope and discover in the second structure malaria parasites. So I take quinine and I get better in the first structure. But also better — or at least, different — in the second structure, as is proved by a second blood slide.

If, however, I regard this recovery in the second structure as the recovery from my illness, I am wrong. For *I* was ill, and only *I* can say of myself or my body that it becomes healthy. This reality of illness or health is something which escapes the microscope. For I cannot say that the observed slide is diseased or that it is healthy. By way of a neutral structure, which is neither healthy nor ill, I pass from illness to health. The relationship between these two structures is obvious, but also obvious is their difference. Between the two structures stands the magnifying glass — and everything connected with it. This takes the object out of its dimensions and takes away its meaning.

The same can be said with respect to the tree infected with mycosis. The slide doesn't show anything of the sick tree or of the healthy tree. One can see the two trees standing there, the healthy, green tree, full of leaves, and next to it the diseased, brownish tree with sparse leaves. One likes to sit down under the former, but not under the latter. The microscopic slide doesn't give any advice in this matter; it is concerned with other things. Nevertheless, the inclination is to sit down under this tree and avoid that one. There is also the fear that the tree which is diseased and rotten will fall. These and other similar intentions, expectations and fears give meaning to the statement that the tree is healthy or diseased. The microscope isolates the tree from such contexts, for it strips the tree of its dimension and, by the same token, deprives it of its meaning and destiny. The cells in themselves have no meaning, but the tree does. That healthy tree there, for instance, in the woods: it is lovely to behold, full of leaves and casts a deep shadow. In all this heat I'd love to lie down under it.

I'd like to rest on that ground with its compact first structure. The ground with molecules and atoms is the second structure. I look above and see there will be a moon and many stars. All this constitutes the first structure. Stars with this or that type of atmosphere and this or that degree of heat are the second structure. I am beginning to understand the kind of world I am living in. My thoughts go back to the baluster on the lawn. The first structure is not constant. The baluster became longer, but above all different. The materiality of that piece of wood which lies so incongruously out there on the grass is different. When I see it there, I can hardly arrive at another judgment. If I were to put the baluster on the pavement of a street, its materiality again would be different. That, too, I would see.

Is it possible for me to change the location of the baluster and, at the same time, leave it in the first structure? More generally expressed, can I change the position of matter without changing it in its first structure? The differences are often small and therefore wouldn't draw attention. Yet the change is real and visible to anyone who is willing to see it. I recall seeing a match stick lying on the entrance steps of the cathedral of Laon. The difference between this match and the one at home in the ashtray was evident;

it disappeared only when I appealed to my belief in the second structure. I certainly believe in that second structure, but I also attach value to the belief in the first structure, the one which I experience everyday and immediately; I don't want to lose this belief.

The baluster out there is longer. Or shorter, depending on its position and its surroundings. At any rate, a meter *here* is never one meter *there* — a formula in which the term "meter" doesn't seem to fit. For the meter, understood in the sense of 100 centimeters — the sense of a measurement that has been fixed once and for all — is the proof of disbelief in the mutability of things. But if I realize that the meter, together with the object to be measured, changes in length, then the term "meter" can be retained.

This is a point I wish to hold on to today in all my further reflections. The length of the measuring rod changes whenever it is moved, in equal measure with the moving of the thing to be measured; thus this thing measured with the rod seemed to retain the same length. At the same time, however, I maintain the rule that the meter, as distance and as measuring length, never possesses the same dimension. I say "never," because the circumstances or conditions also are never the same.

More generally formulated, the rule is: in every change of position the dimension of things changes. Or, again in a more general way and more appropriate terms: in every change in position the materiality of things changes. I can see that here; after its change in position, the baluster has remained wood, but the wood I see is different. The most striking aspect of the difference is the change in dimension. This is often the case, but it manifests itself particularly in the case of the baluster. Nevertheless, I can deny the difference without much effort. All I have to do is to consider the second structure of the wood as more real than the first. Generally speaking, it is possible to deny the above-formulated law or rule through an appeal to the second structure of matter.

It is only in some cases that such a denial becomes difficult or impossible. To investigate this further, let us begin with an example in which the denial is difficult; next we will see an example which makes the denial impossible, in my opinion, for all. The first example I'll take from a personal experience. Here the positions of things were not changed, but I myself had changed my location in the midst of them. For the purpose of testing the above-mentioned rule this change makes no difference.

While I was still a university student I went hiking with a friend from Lugano to Bellinzona. The day was hot — just as hot as it is today. All we had was a bad map, and so we thought that, after going down the slope from Monte Ceneri, we would almost at once arrive at Bellinzona. Instead we found a long straight road, and at the end of it we could see in the distance Bellinzona. We were literally exhausted. That morning, when we left, we were already tired, we had been hiking a whole week already in that same heat, with heavy packs on our backs, marching twenty-five to thirty-five miles a day. Everything had gone wrong on our southerly hike — including expenses. So we were even suffering from hunger. It was no longer any fun.

I still see that long asphalt road stretching out before us, with its unforgettable sign: *Bellinzona 5 km.* Five kilometers, that's one full hour of hiking. But one hour of marching is a lot when one is hungry, thirsty, tired and full of blisters. Besides, ten or fifteen kilometers would have been more honest than the proclaimed five. But even these numbers would not have told the story of the length of that road. In all its concreteness, the road was much longer; that was the way we saw and felt it.

Anyone would have felt the same as we did in similar circumstances. But everyone will also be able to deny the reality of this perceptual extension of the road. It is even beyond doubt that belief in the second structure, which is always present, more or less undoes the extension of the road for the walker. In moments of extreme fatigue, when every new step is like lead, that belief in the second structure gives way to the reality of that long, long road under one's feet. Right now, while I am merely recalling that hike, it's easy for me to deny that reality since I am not tired. But it was an entirely different matter at that time.

Five kilometers! The number made us furious. The little poles at intervals of one hundred meters along the road bed seemed to be set too far apart; moreover, the distance between them was constantly increasing. Since that time I have come to realize that the distances really become greater, that in all reality they are greater. In order to learn about distance, what more realistic way is there than to go on a hike? Thus, within the reality of our hike we knew how long the road was from Lugano to Bellinzona. Any other reality would give another distance. Our blistered feet, the pressing packs on our backs, the heat, the hunger, the thirst and our fatigue — these were the factors that made that distance long.

Perhaps other factors would have made it shorter. Factors are never absent. In order for the length of the road to remain constant, a very large number of factors would have to be fulfilled. The hiker should then be neither well-rested nor exhausted, neither happy nor sad, neither hungry nor satiated, neither lonely nor with others. But there is no such person. Hence our conclusion is that the road has a constant length only if no one travels it. But such a road is meaningless; there is no such road. If no one travels the road, then that road doesn't exist. This is beyond doubt. Thus we can return to the formula that the road is always and without exception different for everyone who becomes acquainted with it, for everyone who studies it and for everyone who walks it; and the road is different for them at every moment.

Moreover, everything on the road and alongside the road is different. The asphalt, the stones, the grass, the dust on the grass, the view, the light — all these change. One who is tired sees a different light from one who is well-rested. Can one rightly claim that the light seen by a well-rested walker is more genuine and more real than that perceived by a tired hiker? If I accept that, then the light — and everything else on and near the road — would be genuine and real only when the walker takes his first step, for no one remains physically fit and well-rested throughout his hike. He who stays fit and well-rested is not walking. One who starts to walk is with his fitness only the beginner of a walk and therefore can be only the beginner of his seeing, appreciating and measuring. By walking he has to make the seeing, appreciating and measuring of the road his own. This means that the light which the tired walker sees is more real for the whole, tiresome road than the light which he saw when he was not yet tired. Before he was tired, the walker saw the light of the start of walking, the light of one hour's at most or perhaps only a few minutes' walking. The light that follows thereafter can be the light of the whole day, that whole day, in which it becomes clear that the road makes him tired.

A long straight road which does not become tiring and boring isn't a long straight road. A mountainous road which doesn't make one gasp for breath isn't a steep road. The first steps, which are taken when we are not yet tired and gasping, don't acquaint us with that road. Only when one becomes tired and begins to gasp does one become acquainted with that road. There are roads which show their true, their real length only when one groans and gasps.

When tired, one sits along such a road; one removes his shoes and socks, stretches out and takes a rest. Then the road becomes different. Later if one has a chance to travel the same road by car, the road is unfamiliar. This happened to me; later I drove back over the road from Lugano to Bellinzona by car and I wasn't able to recognize any of the qualities of the road I had observed when I hiked over it. Five kilometers, said the road sign. Fine; the number appealed to me, for it suits one who isn't tired, and I was fit and in high spirits in that car. Aside from not being tired, if I had been at the same time also unfit and in low spirits, the number five would undoubtedly have appealed even more to me — at least if one can assume that anything can appeal to one who is neither tired nor fit and in high spirits, that is to say, neither tired nor rested. I would then virtually not have been there. The number five is, like all numbers, the number of one who is absent.

This means that the above-formulated law or rule assumes a new form. Let us limit ourselves again to dimensions. At first the rule was: the measure of things changes in position. Now it is: only for those who are absent does the dimension of things remain constant. In practice this means that one who wishes to perceive with constant dimensions must absent himself. Since this is not possible — which implies that constant dimensions are impossible — the rule is that one who wishes to perceive with maximally constant dimensions must absent himself as much as possible.

It *is* possible to absent oneself to a very high degree. One who succeeds in being absent ceases to be tired or rested, thirsty or slaked, hungry or filled; he also ceases to be a friend, enemy, spouse, father, mother, husband, or wife; he almost ceases to be a human being; but it is possible. At any rate, one can try it and be successful; the physical sciences have gloriously proved it. It is even certain that in the past few centuries, and particularly in the past few decades, this removing of oneself from the scene has become something that can be pursued with increasing ease and therefore also with the corresponding degree of success.

Fear, hunger, thirst and exhaustion, a few essential "companions" in measuring a road with which travellers used to be familiar, become increasingly scarcer. One who travels by car may fear a collision, but that fear is of a different kind. Fear, dread even, of distance and of space as such has virtually disappeared. The entire earth has become a map which no longer contains any blank gaps. Roads, cities, restaurants, motels and especially road signs have all become familiar to us. With few exceptions, one who travels by car follows his map. The motorist sits in comfort; he no longer gets blisters on his feet and, as a rule, doesn't suffer from hunger and thirst. That means to a large extent he is absent. All this applies to a motorist, one who can still get tired from his long trip. But today there are also occupations and situations which exclude even this tiredness. More than even before it is easy today to play the absentee and to find the constant dimensions which accompany that condition.

Nevertheless, there are dimensions and sizes which can bring uncertainty even to the most up-to-date, saturated *absentee*. They can make him realize that the impossibility which he experiences when he attempts to deny that those dimensions become longer or shorter applies also to other, less compelling instances of becoming longer or shorter. I am referring here to dimensions and measurements in the vertical direction. My second example will illustrate what I have in mind.

Vertically speaking, all of us suffer from impediments. Climbing a vertical mountain-side presents innumerable difficulties. Mount Everest is only five and one half kilometers high; such a length is horizontally said to be only a short distance, but one can climb it only with the greatest effort. This illustration, however, is still too bodily connected with the old, authentic impediment implied in any change of position. As such, it isn't very suitable to demonstrate that verticality as such has different dimensions. Let us therefore use another example.

In the city of Utrecht, a medieval church tower, called "The Dom," stands on a small square, from which narrow streets go off in various directions. The tower is over 330 feet high. If a child were asked how far the bricks would reach in one of those streets if the tower would suddenly fall down in its full length, he would answer that the rubble would cover one of those streets almost to its full length. The child is mistaken, but even a grown-up would err in his estimate. If he measures out the distance of 330 feet on the ground, he will find that the rubble would barely reach the beginning of one of those streets. What accounts for this difference? The only reason, I think, why the bricks don't go beyond the entrance of the street is that their vertical dimension is longer compared to the same dimension on the horizontal plane. Up there, the bricks are longer. When the tower falls, they shrink.

The bricks shrink when the tower falls. I have to get used to such an idea, of course, but I don't see it as something impossible. What I do see is that it does happen. What falls becomes shorter. The same bricks are horizontally shorter than they were vertically. Is this something that can be checked by using a measuring rod? No, the rod which I take with me while climbing the tower becomes, during and through the climbing, just as much longer as the bricks up there which became longer at the time when the tower was built. In other words, one doesn't notice anything when one is measuring at the top.

Up there one only observes that the tower is high, even higher than it seemed to be below when one suspected that the bricks of the falling tower would hit so far, much too far, down the street. One suspects that the tower, viewed from above, would fall even farther down the street. Does this mean that we are more impeded vertically from the top-down than we are in that same direction upwards? The answer is undoubtedly in the affirmative. To go up we need auxiliary means, for few people can jump higher than a few feet. It is easy, of course, to go down, as we know from painful falls, but no one wishes to go down unassisted; and this is what causes impediments in the vertical downward direction. A fall of a few feet can result in a broken ankle and one of thirty feet can result in death.

If upward verticality is impeded by physical impotence, downward verticality is impeded by danger. And danger apparently is more powerful than impotence. This accounts for the greater elongation of dimensions through danger than through impotence. Anyone can observe this by looking down from a tower. The depth dimension is great, dizzying even for many, but the same distance, measured upward is markedly less; and the same distance seen horizontally would be called short by everyone. It would be instructive to lay out the length of the tower — 330 feet —

in a park; one would then see how much greater are dimensions in the vertical position. That length in a park isn't too far for a little child to stray from his mother. Even in the woods where the distances — the feet — are longer than in a park, one would permit a child to do that. But that same distance of 330 feet, as seen from the top of a tower, becomes bottomless.

If I look up at the tower from below, people up there look small, smaller than people who are 330 feet away on a horizontal plane. This is in agreement with what was said above. Those on the tower are farther away. And if I look down from the tower, the people below on the square are smaller again than those I saw above on the tower. This also is in agreement with my observations. The distance between them and me is greater from above than from below. The tower which is higher through its verticality becomes even higher if I mount it by climbing its stairs.

Thus it is important to make a clear distinction between the two processes involved. The bricks of the tower become longer at the moment when the tower is built. This is the first process, which can be described in this general rule: verticality increases every dimension in the vertical direction. Secondly, the bricks of the tower become longer when one climbs the tower. This is the second process, which can also be described in a general rule: verticality is longer from above than from below.

In the light of this knowledge, so much suddenly becomes clear to me that in my excitement I do not know where to begin with my reflections. Height, depth, distance and nearness — they are the dimensions of our existence. So much happens to us every day within these dimensions. It must be delightful to test the rules we have discovered with respect to all those things and in this way to clarify much of what can be so obscure when we first become acquainted with it. But everything cannot be done at once. Right now as I sit here on the porch, I only wish to clarify the rules; the rest will have to wait.

For everything isn't clear. For example, I am at once intrigued by the following fact. The bricks become vertically larger when they are piled on top of one another. One can see this at the length of the pile and, moreover, observe it when the tower falls. If the pile remains intact and I look at the vertical dimension from above, the same bricks become even longer than they were as viewed from below. While this may be clear, what is not yet clear at all is the fact that the bricks and all other objects which appear longer within the totality of the pile, are nowhere near that length when taken separately; on the contrary, they appear shorter. This point is demonstrated even in the people who from below are seen standing on top of the tower. But let us add another example.

During a storm, the weathercock was blown down from the tower in my home town. The thing crashed onto the pavement below. There were cracks in the cement and the cock itself was also damaged. But that wasn't the first thing people noticed. What struck them the most was the cock's improbable size. Had such a large cock been standing on their tower?, they asked themselves in amazement. Under the above-formulated rules, this amazement must remain. The object — that is, in this case the weathercock — should be large on top of the tower, and therefore, small after landing on the pavement below.

I am not expressing myself in an entirely correct way. According to the rule of elongation in the vertical dimension, the cock shouldn't be larger on top of the tower but only longer in verticality, from foot to crest. By the same rule, the cock should have been shorter below, shorter from foot to crest. But what we saw was a cock which was larger in all its dimensions, most of all from foot to crest. Or, if we look at the size of the cock on the pavement, we find that the one we had been looking at for years on top of the tower was smaller from foot to crest than he appeared to be down on the pavement. How was that possible?

I find the answer in the following way. If objects high up are larger in their vertical dimension than below — and this is beyond doubt — then the highest objects, through the elongated dimensions of all bricks below them, are most distant from us; hence they are not larger but *smaller*. The same principle applies on the horizontal plane. A man who walks away from us becomes smaller until, within the boundaries of his own dimensions, he even becomes lost in the scenery. What I saw on the pavement at the foot of the tower was a cock that had returned from a great distance and therefore had become large, that is enlarged by his fall.

Moreover, because the crest of the cock had returned from a greater height than its foot, the entire figure of the cock had been elongated; in addition, the distance from the crest to the foot was even greater than could have been expected within the generally enlarged proportions. This last-named point can also be expressed a little differently. The cock came from high up; every difference in height — and therefore also the difference in height from below to the foot and from below to the crest — exercises influence on the distance of the farthest point — that is, in this case, the crest — for this reason the cock became most elongated from foot to crest when he fell. This means that there are not two but three processes; therefore also not two but three rules governing the dimensions of vertically placed objects. These processes and rules can be summarized as follows.

The first process is that all objects placed in the vertical direction become longer in that direction. The rule flowing from this process is: high up all objects are longer in the vertical direction than they are on the ground.

The second process is that objects placed in the vertical direction become longer again when one moves upward in their verticality. This gives rise to the second rule; the vertical dimension of objects is larger from above than from below.

The third process that objects which move away from us become smaller, and the corresponding rule is: at a distance all objects are smaller. This process and rule are equally valid on the horizontal level.

It was this third rule that made the weathercock below larger than high up, although the first rule had made us suspect that the cock would be smaller. The same rule underlies the fact that the fallen cock was most strongly elongated from feet to crest, while precisely this distance should have been proportionately smaller according to the first rule. The third rule apparently prevails over the first: the process which makes the falling cock become smaller fades into insignificance beside the process that makes him become larger.

Does the third rule always prevail over the first? Much appears to argue in favor of this. In that case there is a fourth rule, viz., the third process is more powerful than the first. This rule obliges architects to design the higher windows in a tower in such a way that they are longer than the lower windows but equal in breadth. If he makes all windows equal in length, then the higher windows become, according to the fourth rule, too short, so that the tower loses height. Giotto's campanile in Florence, with its ever longer windows toward the top is a very useful and beautiful illustration of this fourth rule.

A few simple experiments can clarify the first rule. I have a writingpad with blank, slightly transparent paper. I put the pad up on its bottom edge and with my pencil I draw a square as accurately as possible, guided only by eyesight. I then perforate the upper corners with a needle in such a way that the next sheet also is punctured. After turning over the page, I put the pad horizontally on the table and, starting from the two needle marks, I draw another square on the second sheet, again guided only by eye-sight. I do my very best to make the sides as equal as possible. Finally I turn the first sheet back over the second, so that the two squares are in the same position. The transparency of the paper allows me to see both squares. I can then see that the bottom of the first square which I drew in a vertical position lies inside the second horizontally drawn square. This proof shows that even on a small scale such as a writingpad dimensions become larger when they are put in a vertical position. But I have to note here that I mustn't pay too much attention to the change which the size of the writingpad itself undergoes when I modify its position. If I take that change into account, then the two squares become less evidently different.

There is, moreover, another, more important matter to which I should pay attention. Books and newspapers with their numerous pictures have taught me to see horizontally things that exist only vertically. For instance, I have often seen that famous medieval church tower of Utrecht flat on my desk; yet only a picture on the wall would be adequate. The effect of years of horizontal seeing consists in the fact that everything which is really vertical — particu-

larly, everything vertical which remains within the dimension of a newspaper or a book — more or less assumes the
meaning and therefore also the dimensions of the horizontal.
This can not happen in the case of that tower; it is too high;
the tower outside cannot possibly be seen horizontally, no
matter how óften I have seen it flat on my table in a book
or paper. But in the case of a little square which I myself
draw on a piece of paper it is very easy to see and interpret
horizontally what one has drawn vertically. This, of course,
would spoil the effect of the experiment. After this warning
it becomes possible to perform the next experiment.

The pencil with which I have drawn the squares lies flat
on the table before me. It is black, thin object with a certain length. How long? I take a small ruler, the kind school
boys use, and estimate the length of the pencil, by merely
putting my thumb on the ruler, without placing the ruler
alongside the pencil and without reading the markings on
the ruler. At the spot where my estimating thumb touches
the ruler I put a mark on the latter with another pencil.
Next, I place the first pencil in a vertical position and again
estimate its length, without putting it alongside the ruler,
reading the latter's markings, or — and this is of special importance here — without changing the position of the ruler
in my hand. In other words, if in my first estimate of the
pencil's length the ruler was in a horizontal position, I continue to keep it horizontally. The result will then be that
my second estimate is greater, provided I take care not to
see "horizontally," and this may not be easy, as should be
clear from the warning given above. But if I overcome this
difficulty, then the following experiment can serve to further
test the rules we have found.

A small piece of the lead protrudes from the pencil which
lies horizontally before me. I slowly move the pencil from

the horizontal to the vertical position, paying attention to the protruding lead. This lead becomes longer while I am looking at it, as it should according to the first rule. For obvious reasons the third rule, which could eliminate the first, isn't involved here. If, next, I slowly return the pencil to its horizontal position, the piece of lead diminishes in size. In short, the elongation in the change from the horizontal to the vertical position, as well as the corresponding shortening in the shift from the vertical to the horizontal, manifests itself even within the dimensions of a pencil.

But it is very easy not to see this shrinking and stretching of the lead and therefore also to deny them. If I see the pencil as being in principle a little horizontal stick, as, so to speak, the image of the pencil on the horizontal plane, then the elongation and shortening do not occur. Now that I take care not to do that, I see not only the lengthening and shortening of the pencil but I also notice that the pencil, as a whole, becomes longer in its movement toward the vertical position and shorter when it moves from the vertical toward the horizontal. This means that something which first, as in the experiment with the squares, I could read on the writingpad as the result of the change in position, I can now see happen before in the form of the original, length-changing movement. All this is in accordance with the first rule.

To terminate this experiment by way of a summary, I can still verify all this with my measuring tape. I measure the pencil first horizontally and then vertically. I find the same size, of course; this does not surprise me since the tape expands and contracts as I move its position. But now I place the tape alongside the horizontal and then the vertical side of the square which I have drawn in a vertical position. I read the figures nine and ten — nine centimeters

for the vertical side and ten for the horizontal side; the
two figures are unequal because the tape stretches vertically, so that less centimeters are needed for the dimension
which horizontally is ten. If I care I can repeat this procedure with respect to the pencil. The result is the same;
it doesn't contradict the previous result. Much of what used
to be obscure to me now becomes intelligible, particularly,
the following point, which has puzzled me for years.

On the basis of the rules governing dimensions in the
vertical and the horizontal directions, the sun high in the
sky must be smaller than the sun on the horizon. As a matter of fact, this is so; the difference is even striking. One
would estimate that the sun on the horizon is at least two
or three times as large as the sun high in the sky. In this
respect it makes no difference whether one makes the comparison with the rising or the setting sun on the horizon,
although in other respects these two suns are strikingly
different. The difference in size is more easily observed
in the case of the moon because the moon high in the sky
doesn't blind us. But the phenomenon is the same because
the process involved is the same.

It is easy to describe this process. The sun and the moon
which approach the horizon are closer; they enter more
into our horizontal world and thereby become larger. The
same process occurs here as with the weather-cock on the
tower. It was much larger on the pavement below than on
the tower above. If it is put back on the tower, it becomes
small again when seen from below. Now, when we see the
sun rise, it too becomes smaller according to the same rules.
For the same reason also constellations are larger near the
horizon than elsewhere in the sky. The stars scatter at the
horizon because the distances separating them there become
larger. Dimensions on the horizon are dimensions near to

us and therefore have a certain priority. This can be better expressed by saying that the constellations decrease in size overhead because the distances separating the stars become smaller. All this is rather simple and raises no special difficulties.

Difficulties arise when one takes pictures of the constellations, the sun and the moon at different positions in the sky and then discovers that the differences in size observed with the eye have disappeared in the photographs. A photograph of the sun near the horizon and one of the sun high in the sky do not reveal the slightest difference in size. The same applies to the moon; and likewise to the dimensions of constellations, photographed near the horizon as well as high in the sky.

This easily leads to the opinion that the sun, moon and constellations on the horizon are only seemingly enlarged. One is, so it is said, the victim of an optical illusion and one can recognize his mistake by looking at two series of photographs, for the latter show the same dimensions. But such a procedure is not without objections. As far as the sun is concerned, one sees in the photograph a circular spot less than one quarter inch in diameter. May we decide by means of such a small, dimensionally reduced sun what should be said about the size of the sun as such? Caution is to be exercised especially with respect to dimensions. If we photograph two poles that are of different heights against a neutral background, it can happen that the two poles show the same lengths on the photograph because the taller pole was farther away from the camera; yet no one would doubt their difference in length when he looks at the real poles. The distance to the camera was eliminated, and precisely this distance made us certain about their difference in height.

Exactly the same occurs with respect to the sun. The sun at the horizon is visibly near, and the sun high in the sky is visibly far away. The photograph takes away this difference and shows two equal suns. It does this in a very simple way. The photograph makes a horizontal spot of the sun high in the sky, and it does the same with the sun on the horizon. While one wishes to know how much the high sun differs from the low sun, the picture puts both suns low and together. Obviously, they will be equal in that case. But I would be mistaken if I wished to apply the result of this procedure to the real sun. This same objection holds also for the moon and the constellations.

We have spoken of the sun, the moon and constellations, of bricks in a tower and the weather-cock. Vertically dimensions are longer, so that all objects high up are smaller. Every upward relocation of an object makes it smaller because every upward relocation is an enlarged or elongated change in position. But not only upward relocation changes an object's dimensions. Every change in position modifies every object in all its properties, within the limits set by the object itself. The man who walks away from me becomes smaller within his dimensions, or taller in an exceptional context. The baluster out there on the grass has become longer through such an exceptional context, longer than it was when it was lying in front of me on the table.

I have not yet paid much attention to these contexts, which influence or determine so many properties of so many data, objects and persons. This summer afternoon which invites me to meditate, can give me the peace and the desire needed to fill this deficiency. I have the desire and the afternoon is still long. Nobody will disturb me for a while, so I'll have the necessary peace and quiet. And before me I see an enchanting landscape of miscellaneous things in a long, variegated collection of ever new contexts.

COLORS

The weather has changed. The small airy clouds above the trees, which mark the end of the meadow in the distance have grown vastly. They are moving. If I keep perfectly still I can see them grow. But they are not clearly distinguishable because the air is hazy. There is hardly any difference between the clouds and the rest of the sky. All of it seems to be overcast, but right above me there are no clouds. The sky has a yellowish tint. Is there going to be a thunderstorm? With that kind of a sky one can expect a tornado. There is no breeze and it is oppressive. The plants on the border of the meadow are drooping. The leaves on the trees behind the lawn are shiny.

Everything before me looks different. The grass has assumed soft-tinted colors; the flowers have a pinkish hue; the horizon above the meadow is vague and finely tinted; the trees in the distance are subdued and bluish. All colors have turned soft, whitish, yellowish, here and there a mellow red or blue; and above them the pale yellow masses of clouds gathering in a yellow sky. A breath of wind touches the trees; their leaves gently move. I can feel the touch of the wind on my cheeks. A dry leaf rustles across the floor of the porch. The wind dies down again. Everything is motionless and seems to be waiting for something to happen.

Only the clouds are moving; new heads grow out of their core in ferment. Yet, the clouds scarcely increase in size. Something is working up to a climax in the silent but turbulent masses. A few drops of rain fall from the cloudless sky above me. But the sky is covered with a misty veil. I can look at the sun without being blinded. The sun is a dull red in a yellowish, veiled and closed sky. Together, the garden, the woods, the meadow and the distant land form a harmony of colors and shapes. Although this harmony is not the same as that of a bright sun in a blue sky, it is a harmony no less.

Just as the grass and the flowers, the meadow and the distant land, with their subdued veiled colors and vague contours fit in with the yellowish sky and the dull, red sun, so the fresh, brilliant colors and sharp outlines harmonize with the blue sky and the bright light of a blinding sun. There is always harmony in every season, at every hour of the day. The evening colors harmonize with the setting sun; the color of things fits in with the rising sun in the morning; shades and contours of everything adapt themselves to the winter, as a landscape in the snow or a snow-covered street. Always, down to the last detail, there is a harmonious whole. As is the case here before me, below the red sun.

The sun is red, of course, because the sky is hazy. I know the phenomenon very well. If I look at the sun through the smoke coming from a chimney, it is also red. When trains were still pulled by steam-engines, I would often stand along the track to see the sun change its color through the puff of smoke. During World War II, after the burning of Rotterdam, when charred bits of paper fell from the sky, the sky was also yellow and the sun had the same red color. An ominous sun shone on a sinister event. Today, too, the sun scarcely looks reassuring, but not in the same way. What is being spawned there in the distance? Red is the color of danger, but only this red, not the red of flowers. Even the red sun can be safe. When the sun sets it is red, and nothing is as peaceful as a setting sun.

The sunset offers a world of colors. The sky, which has been blue all day long, assumes the most surprising colors. Overhead, the blue becomes ever more intense and ultimately almost black. On the horizon where the sun will set, the sky becomes red, first pink to orange, then deep-red and in that red, there is a large somewhat flattened, flaming red sun. But no trace of any danger. There is nothing between me and the sun, nothing impure, nothing threatening. The air is perfectly clear. But the redness which is seen now is caused by impurities such as dust or perhaps even by a disaster somewhere between me and the sun. The sun itself with its ominous glow proves this. But the redness of the setting sun is of a different kind. What does this redness mean? The harmony of a sunset is meaningful. Above me, is a deep-blue, dark sky and near the sunset there is a brilliant sky in which there are fanlike or thin, elongated clouds assuming ever new colors until they finally perish in a flaming red. And in this sky is a somewhat flattened, huge, red sun. There is unity in all this, but what is it? This lead me to my second meditation.

Second Reflection

If I try to find words to express what the red of the setting sun means, I may not throughout my inquiry lose sight of the fact that the red setting sun belongs to the totality indicated by the term "sunset." The reasons are obvious. In the first place, no one witnesses a segregated red sun; one always sees scenery under the setting sun; for instance, a sea over which the sun sets. Now, my topic is concerned with the red of the sun in its concrete setting and I must stick to my subject.

The second reason is connected with the first. It is this: now that I wish to investigate what influence the whole or the context exercises on the detail, I would frustrate my intention by lifting the detail out of the totality. One could object that the separation of the detail from the whole should leave that detail largely, if not completely, intact. But this is not so. Everything I see here around me points to the contrary. That baluster is different, within the limits of its nature, by virtue of the context in which it is situated. Nothing remains of the context's influence if I take the baluster out of the totality through my way of looking at it and thinking about it. The same happens with respect to the redness of the sun. If the sun is taken separately, this color means nothing; it could then just as well be blue or green.

But in the totality of the sunset that color is meaningful and needed. (I still have to indicate in what this need for the red color consists.) It is difficult, if not impossible, to let our imagination integrate a green or blue sun in the evening panorama. One who does this, has removed the typical aspect of a sunset from his imagination. The same principle applies to all properties and characteristics of the sunset. The orange of vapor ribbons and streaks in the sky is, taken by itself, fortuitous and meaningless, but in the totality of the sunset this color is meaningful and needed. In short, if I wish to indicate what I see, then I must maintain the unity of what is presented to me. Now, what is this unity? What is the unity in which the sun is red?

Even before I find the answer, I know that this answer mustn't be far-fetched. For the unity which I see is accessible, simple and easy to enjoy, so that it should also be easy to understand or at least to express. I retract the term "to understand," for it is too loaded, too much related to a laborious and involved process of thinking to indicate what is demanded of me when I wish to say what the sunset contains. The answer to this question, then, can be given at once. The panorama of the sunset is the panorama of the *evening*. The evening is a totality, in which the sun is red. The color of the sun is the red of the evening.

What have I gained with this seemingly trivial answer? The evening — is that all? Indeed, that is all. If only it were given to me to say what the evening is! I wish that I could express what I experience, what everybody experiences, when the evening is closing in. Every moment of the day has in all simplicity its own grandeur. The evening brings the day to a close and shrouds whatever happiness or sorrow the day has brought. The evening, which brings peace to the impetuous heart, has descended upon every battlefield throughout mankind's warlike history. This is the dusk that one day will settle over each one of us at death. The ever-recurrent consolation in man's always dissatisfied, always rebelling, always seeking and doubting existence. The ever-recurring affirmation of the moment of bliss.

You are right; I am not a poet — nor do I wish to be a

poet. What I wish to do is introduce words like those above into science, which is so indigent in this matter. These would be words more carefully pondered, more serenely formulated and better considered. If events or things act on our emotions, or at least strike us, why should this aspect be so consistently passed over in silence? I protest against this distortion of reality, and this protest is embodied in my method. Let me now try to determine what is contained in the red color of the setting sun. The answer, again, will be simple.

The evening is the end of the day, and this is what I see in the sunset. I don't see it as a flashing moment but as the last phase of the time period "day." I see the day at the moment when it becomes evening; I witness the completion of the process called "day," the main phases of which are morning, noon, and evening. The morning, which I greeted from behind my desk or which I slept through so deliciously or so miserably, comes to its end over there. That morning's sun is being extinguished over there. So also is the heat of this day's sun dying out there; in that dimming red glow the sun loses its power and tension. It even sags a little. What? The sun sags a little? That is an unexpected discovery, one that deserves to be considered more closely for a few moments, after which we will return to our topic.

The sun is a celestial body, about one million miles away from us and having a diameter that is more than one hundred times that of the earth; only two billionth of its radiation reaches the earth, etc., etc. Within the context of such facts — which I cannot and do not wish to deny — the statement that the sun sags a little in the evening on the horizon because its power is gone, is naive, ridiculous, and unbelievable. But I am not seeking and speaking now within the context of the second structure. In principle I know about this context, but it does not help me now as I look at the sun.

Once upon a time I used to think differently; unsurprisingly, I used to be enraptured — and still am — by the enormous, ingeniously acquired knowledge of the sun and of so many other things which man has gathered in the second structure. But every time I looked at the sun and many other things, that knowledge remained distant, strange and incredible. Incredible in a different sense, however, than the one concerned with the sun sagging a little in the evening, and it is precisely in this different sense that I am searching today. Does the statements that the sun sags a little fit into that context, that is, the content of the first structure?

It certainly does, but on one condition. The sun is undoubtedly flat on the horizon, and the flatness of the sun just as undoubtedly gives me the impressions that the day is over as far as the sun is concerned. However, this statement is not sufficient, it still needs amplification. Let anyone amplify it as he wishes, but whatever explanation is given, the fact that the flattening of the sun harmonizes with the fact of the evening must be preserved. The fire has gone out of the sun; anyone can see that. Later we will return to this point, but let us now return to our topic, viz., the red color of the setting sun.

I am trying to imagine what I would see if a green or blue sun, rather than a red one, were shining in the flaming distance. With such a sun could I still believe in the evening? A green or blue sun would be in conflict with the completion of the day which announces itself everywhere else. Evening and red belong together, but not merely because we have associated them in our experience over many years. That unity cannot be observed in me but in the sky. Isn't it true that everything which flames and glows dies out in redness? The sun is no exception to this rule. It has happened, on the horizon, the day is past, the light extinguished. When the daylight fades, the sun becomes red. No one can expect it to be green, blue or white.

In the morning the sun is also red, and large and somewhat flattened. None of these three properties which the rising sun shares with the setting sun is out of place. When the new, large sun rises above the landscape in the morning, it is neither fully radiant, nor full of power, nor even a perfectly round sun. But these properties are not entirely the same as the corresponding properties of the setting sun. For example, the rising sun usually is not as large as the setting sun. Isn't the rising sun just as close? This is, indeed, the effect it creates; and it is good in a mediation such as this one to hold on to an experience that isn't yet handicapped by anything. In the morning the sun is still too fresh to be as close to us as it is in the evening, for then it has been our companion also all day long.

Because of this same freshness the morning sun also gives less light than the evening sun. However, it undoubtedly gives more light than the evening sun at the same altitude. This, too, can be understood. The rising sun attains the full light of the day speedily; it has the drive of one who is just starting. The evening sun, on the other hand, lingers and then slowly fades away. In my opinion, this is also the reason for the red of the evening sun being darker than that of the rising sun. The redness of the morning sun is different; it is somewhat like an enamel, while the setting

sun is like velvet. My choice of words is poor, not only because it is difficult to express what one sees, but particularly because I am in danger of disregarding the warning
I gave myself at the beginning of the mediation. I said
there that I did not wish to describe any property separately
from the totality in which it occurs.

If I wish to know what the sun's color is at dawn and at
dusk, then I must go out into the open fields or into a suitable city square, and observe the conditions of the sun's
color. This color then is dependent on everything that is
in that spot. While the sun projects one color, one size
and one flatness above the sea, at the same moment that
same sun projects a different size and a different flatness
above a turbulent city. It is hardly possible, of course, to
be in two places at the same time. But one who is used to
watching the sun knows better than to make a judgment
about it in isolation, for he knows from experience that the
sun is different in different places. Even small details are
significant. For example, the sun's color in the morning is
different when there has been dew. Neither of these two
colors, however, can claim any priority; both are real as
the many other colors which the sun assumes in other
conditions.

This kind of observation should lead to caution in the
use of instruments in measuring the color of the sun. Let
us dwell a little on this point. First of all, the instrument
cannot possibly take into account the circumstances — circumstances of which the sun itself is both the proof and
the illustration. The instrument measuring colors doesn't
register the morning or the evening, that is, the moment
of the investigation. The instrument causes the researcher
to investigate the morning sun without the morning, the

evening sun without the evening, etc. The result of this is that fewer colors are registered with the aid of the instrument than with the naked eye. With the instrument the color of the rising sun is barely different from that of the setting sun at the same altitude, an effect which seems unbelievable, but which nonetheless must be accepted as soon as one takes the sun out of the total context.

Taken separately, the sun on the horizon isn't large. An instrument used in measuring the sun doesn't take the sun's position in the sky into account. It removes the time element from the event, and what is an event without time? It is an event that doesn't happen. No one can expect the sun to change much in an event that doesn't happen. But what is surprising is the fact that the sun can adapt itself so well to the instrument with respect to its color and that it adapts itself fully to the instrument with respect to its dimensions. The instrument, which makes things stable and, by the same token, almost makes us forget how much they change, in this way helps us realize that things do change and that they even change considerably. The instrument makes this contribution in the following way. If one removes the element of the morning time and the evening time, then the two sums are equal. The instrument makes this important "reduction"; it removes the evening from the evening and the morning from the morning. When this is done, the things of both time periods — in this case the evening sun and the morning sun — show that they can adapt themselves to this "reduction." They are then equal or nearly equal; they have been able to go through the change toward equality almost completely.

I say "almost completely," for the two suns are not *entirely* equal, as measured with the instrument, except for their size. The immense sun on the horizon in the morning and the even larger sun on the horizon in the evening reveal themselves fully equal. They are equal also to the so much smaller sun high in the sky. But the color of the two suns remains unequal, although the inequality established by the instrument is only a fraction of what the eye sees. Where does this slight variation come from? Not from the two suns, for that would mean that the sun changes – a supposition which, as a matter of principle, must be rejected from the standpoint of the instrument. The difference must therefore lie outside the two suns; in this case, in the atmosphere, the properties of which are unequal in the morning and the evening. They are not equal, however, because of a change in the atmosphere as such – that, too, is inadmissible – but because the concentration of dust particles in the atmosphere increases or decreases.

In this way there arises a consistent reasoning process which keeps things stable because the postulate of immutability is preserved from the beginning to the end. The unequal always lies "somewhere else," and it is ultimately never really unequal but merely a shift in degree or percentage. Degrees and percentages can be measured. Equality leads to measuring, even to constant measuring, and terminates in a comprehensive whole of ever gradual but constant facts, all of which belong to the second structure of matter. This second structure has been drawn from matter by the instrument. Things apparently permit this.

Things permit quite a few things in the second structure. For example, the sun permits light which is equally white in the morning, at noon, in the evening and even at night to be broken up by the spectrograph into numerous colors. In the spectrum one can distinguish lightless lines which indicate the elements present in the atmosphere around the sun. The concentration of these elements can be measured. Because of such instruments there arose a science which teaches us innumerable details about the sun, which are a delight to know. In another sense it is also a delight to learn about details present in the reality of the first structure of the sun, details which everyone sees when the sun shines, sets and rises over a landscape. These details also can be gathered together to constitute a science.

To perceive colors is a matter of the moment; I see this here in the garden. Now that the weather is changing, every moment the colors are different. However, I do not think that it will end in a thunderstorm. Whenever I gaze at the garden the colors are new. And the sky changes from moment to moment above the garden. Would it be possible for me to catch the color above the lawn with an instrument, that is, with a color film? The question is important now that color photographs, color movies, color slides and color television represent such moments and it is *tacitly* assumed that the colors one sees in this way agree with the true colors and are even identical with them.

What are we to say of a color photo? Certainly the color representation is beautiful, but the colors are not genuine. The representation is a picture, a beautiful picture, too beautiful even, for things weren't like that. Where is the difference then? The question is all the more important when one rightly observes that the colors change from moment to moment and that the picture freezes one of these moments. There are several reasons for the above-mentioned difference.

First of all, the moment mentioned in the statement that colors change from moment to moment isn't equal to the moment of the photograph. The former shares in the day, the latter does not. With my eye I see the here and now, but this isn't the same as the fragment which I cut with my camera — one hundredth of a second — out of a uniform, equably passing time. With respect to seeing, time does not pass equably. Occasionally time goes fast, but then at other times it goes slow. When a gust of wind whipped through the leaves, time went fast; but it went fast only in the leaves. When I see the clouds moving in the sky, another and faster time prevails. The camera cannot record these differences. Even a movie doesn't really give a true picture of what the things in the landscape show with respect to time. But with a certain amount of good will one can make time out of that. It can even be done with a simple photograph, but then considerable leniency is required.

Other matters also are relevant with respect to colors. A color photograph of a landscape or an interior produces a strange, pop-art like effect, but this isn't only because the moment of the eye has been replaced by the moment of a shutter. This substitution is common to the color photo and the black and white picture; yet the latter doesn't create that artificial effect, at least not to the same extent. What gives the color photograph that artificiality, which doesn't exist in a good painting? One who looks closely at a painting will see that the artist used a surprising variety of colors, undoubtedly intended to express reality as he saw it. Does that reality possess those colors? Yes and no. Let us explain why.

To be more explicit, let us assume that the artist has painted two equal objects, two pewter mugs, at different locations on his canvas. Viewed from a distance, the two objects are equally grey. One stands on a table covered with a purple cloth. On close inspection it appears that this pewter mug has not been painted grey but green. The other stands on a yellow-brown floor and, seen from nearby, it proves to be blue. But, viewed from a distance, both objects are grey, and equally so. If I carefully inspect the two mugs on the canvas, I see that the artist didn't simply paint them blue and green but used a variety of colors. Amidst the green is some purple and white and amidst the blue is some red and green. Yet from a distance the effect given is an even grey.

If the artist had painted both pewter mugs a solid grey, they wouldn't have looked grey. In fact, they would have differed in color. However, if the mugs had been standing here on the table, they would in all reality have been a solid grey. This means that when they are arranged in different positions — for instance, the two positions which the artist saw and laid down on canvas — they change color. They change color while they remain equal in color.

Now that I know this, I can see it also in the objects here. The lawn is equally green in all places. At the same time, the grass has a different color in different places. Here I see it yellow, there brown, elsewhere orange; and where the grass is shaded, it is blue. Nevertheless, there remains an overall impression of one homogeneously green field. If I wish to paint this field homogeneously green, I will need many other colors in addition to green. The color photograph is unable to express all this; at most it can represent some of the differences, such as the intensity of the green and the differences in color where a shadow lies. But the camera cannot capture the complex interplay of colors as such which the lawn performs in the totality of the landscape. For example, the color photograph cannot capture the nuance of color which the grass close to the baluster possesses. The baluster is out of place in the totality of the garden, and this fact lies anchored in that nuance of color.

One who has planned the color scheme of his room with

care will see that all colors in the room change at the same time when he suddenly replaces the ivory-colored table cover by a red cloth. All the other colors show that the color of the cloth clashes with them; they try, as it were, to disgrace that color. The same disharmony arises sometimes from the mere presence of a small object with the wrong color, so that one has to locate the origin of the dissonant element.

Colors are not stable; yet one at a time they remain consistent. The contradiction here is similar to the one concerned with dimensions. Dimensions aren't stable either; yet one at a time they remain consistent. The baluster on the grass is not erratically larger, but only within the limit of its own dimension; the man who walks away becomes smaller within his own dimension. He really becomes smaller, as visual experience tells us, but remains consistent with himself in length, as the same visual experience tells us. The stone which is changed from a horizontal to a vertical position becomes longer in that direction, but its own dimension is still maintained. There is nothing erratic in all this. It would be erratic if the stone were to become ten times or a hundred times as long is the vertical position. One would not be able to live in a world in which such things happened; one couldn't move around in it or build something.

The same holds true for colors. If colors changed arbitrarily, the world would be a polychromatic chaos. A buttercup is yellow and remains yellow. A blue buttercup wouldn't be called a buttercup. But the buttercup has many variations of yellow here and there; that is, its yellow color in the garden differs from its color on the table, or in a well-arranged border as opposed to the yellow color in the city dump. It varies to such an extent that the artist may have to paint it blue in order to prove how yellow that buttercup has remained on this particular spot.

As in the case of dimensions, a rule can also be formulated for colors. It is this: within the limits of its own color any object can, in principle, possess all colors. This rule flows from the process of change in position, regardless of whether the object itself is relocated or the observer assumes a new position. One who changes the position of an object changes its color. If one assumes a new location, then the rule is: he who changes his position changes the color of things. Usually the change is small, so small even that attention has to be drawn to it before one notices it; and sometimes even then one doesn't see it.

But the change can also be big. If one moves from the sunny side to the shady side of a square, all colors become clearly different, and especially those in the shade. At first, when one stood in the sun, the colors of objects in the shade were bluish and lavender hues. But, on moving into the shade, one sees the same objects as yellow, brown or red. None of the colors seen, whether from a position in the sun or from one in the shade, have any priority. For where is the shade more shady, where one can see it from the sunny side or where one stands in it? In the same way the colors of objects in the shade, as seen from both positions, are equally genuine. In spite of all the differences, the color of any object remains consistent.

With respect to colors in the shade there is still another rule that is connected with the one formulated above. The art of painting can again provide an example leading to that rule. A beginner is inclined to make the shadow of the object he paints more or less black. The result of this, however, is disappointing. The painted object then shows no shadow but only a separate black stroke, making the object look as if it consisted of two parts. The real object doesn't have these two parts, but is, in its division of color and light, a unit; everywhere it shows the same color. A face, for example, is always and everywhere flesh-colored, no matter how a shadow falls over it. If the artist wishes to portray the shadow of a face on his canvas, then he will have to paint every area of the painted face in flesh-colors. How he manages this is his own secret; perhaps he uses yellow, green or blue, but if he ever uses black it will be an exception.

Black is a rare color, and pure black hardly occurs or probably doesn't exist at all. If the artist wishes to paint black, he uses colors; and if he uses black he blends it with colors. Black is like white, a collective term. The shade is black, admittedly so; but how many colors does not this black consist of with respect to any object? Coal is black, regardless of the green, the blue, the red and even the yellow that shines in it and which together constitute the black of coal. The night is black, we say, but is the night really black? It has all colors except black. Can this statement be true? It contradicts at least the undeniable fact that the night *extinguishes all colors.* Let us say a few words about this matter.

In the moonlight all objects lose their colors. Walking through a field full of flowers in the moonlight, one sees that all colors have vanished. The light-colored flowers are grey, and the dark ones black. Corn-poppies are black, and so is the grass. Strange as it may seem, one has to intentionally look for this before actually seeing it. The black poppies appear indeed to be black, but one never saw these flowers that way before. What color did the poppy have in the moonlight before one was told that its color was black? It was red, just as red as during the day, and the only thing special was that this permanently red poppy stood, at that moment of perception, in the light of the moon.

The young man who kisses the lips of his girl in the moonlight does not kiss black lips but red lips. True, the red of lips in the moonlight is different, just as everything else about the girl is different in the moonlight; otherwise he wouldn't have any desire to walk with her in the moonlight. That same girl is different in the moonlight; for it is as she is then that her lover wishes to know her, with those special red lips evoked by the moon. In a similar way the red of the poppy reveals a different aspect of the same red color.

Grass remains green at night. Or should I say that my knowledge of the grass' color remains green? In that case I would not look with surprise at the grass when I am told that in the moonlight grass is black, just as black as poppies are. I don't rectify my knowledge but my perception. After I have been told about the blackness of the grass in the moonlight, it doesn't look real to me. But this unbelievable thing is true, though with the one important proviso that time is kept out of the perception. Grass is a matter of a whole day, a year, a whole life even and perhaps centuries. The night on that grass is the night of a whole day and the day on the grass is the day of a year. This is grass, which is green in the spring, yellow in the summer and brown in the autumn. The grass which I see this morning, this noon and this night, the night of this day of this year, is green.

Generally speaking, this second rule applies: the color of every object is consistent at every moment of the day and under every form of illumination. The first rule was that in principle every object has all colors. Formulated in this way, the two rules contradict each other. But to the first rule a condition was attached, viz., *within the limits of its own color,* every object has, in principle, all colors. The green of grass may be blue, yellow, red or even, with the above-mentioned restriction, black, but it remains green, green as grass. This first rule is concerned with the changing of things; it is a rule of the moment. The second rule is a rule of duration.

Things endure, as is manifest in their lasting properties, not the least of which is their lasting color. If things did not endure, then grass would indeed now be green, then blue, and at night really black.

My expressions are not yet cautious enough. By saying "now" and "then," I seem to imply that time as such exists and that we live and things last in this autonomous medium called "time." But the only thing real around us and of us is matter. If things didn't last, time wouldn't exist. Time as such can neither be experienced nor described. This is the reason why all reflections on time as such have always led nowhere and still lead nowhere. Reflection on time as such is reflection in a vacuum. Time exists in the clouds above the meadow, in the flower border around the lawn and in the red sun; in short, it exists in things and in our body. Now, the fact that time has a duration here and there manifests itself in the properties of this here and there, the properties of the things present here and there, their materiality, their dimensions, their changing clarity and their color. Or still more precisely expressed, time is the consistency of the properties of things in spite of all their changes. Or again, to use a formula that still needs to be more closely examined, time is the change of the properties of things, in spite of their consistency.

Time as *tempo* is the changing of things. Time as *period,* as *duration,* is the identity of each thing and of each human body. These words give a new and more general formulation to the rules.

The sun offers an ever-recurring, impressive example of the relationship expressed in these rules. The setting sun is red, flattened and large; its color, shape and dimensions have changed. Nevertheless, the sun is the same sun that shines during the day. If we didn't see an enduring sun, that is, if the sun wasn't lasting in itself, the scene of the setting sun would be less peaceful and perhaps even frightening. Such a giant, blood-red and flattened sun would alarm us by these properties. But this isn't the case. We see the sun which was shining all day long or which we had missed all day long. This same sun is red, flat and large on the horizon. Its color, shape and dimensions remain consistent; the sun has duration.

Let us briefly summarize these three special properties of the sun again, in order to include other points in our meditation. First of all, the sun is red. The sun which shone high above us slowly dims. The process called "sunlight" which encompasses the day, reaches a fitting ending on the horizon. This takes away the alarming aspect which the red sun as such would have. The sun on the horizon is the same brilliant, blinding, white, hot sun that also fades away there. A similar description applies to the rising sun which is also red-colored. The new sun that begins to glow and gets ever more fiery and vermillion or scarlet above the horizon, is the sun which will shine with a blinding light throughout the day and which, if the weather is favorable, will slowly fade away in the darkest red.

Secondly, the sun is large. The sun which was small high up at the great distance of any vertical dimension, becomes larger below, near to us. The swelling sun, which taken as a separate phenomenon, would alarm us, is familiar to us by the process which encompasses the day. Just as familiar as is the rising sun, which initiates that process. The high sun is far, hot and blinding; it cannot be looked at and therefore is, in a sense, unknown. Many people hardly know how small the sun really is up there high in the sky. The sun they know is the sun of the evening and that of the morning. Instead of saying that the sun on the horizon swells beyond its dimensions, it is correct to state that the sun in that place possesses within its dimensions the sizes which fit it best and which are more suitable to it than the sizes high in the sky. The shape and size of the sun are those it has in the evening and the morning above the horizon. But this shape and size are preserved in the sun when it stands high in the sky. The period called "day," which the sun itself controls and demarcates, keeps it consistent in size.

Thirdly, the sun is flat. The horizontal diameter of the setting sun, as well as that of the rising sun, is greater than its vertical counterpart. The difference is clear and not disturbing. The sun's shape would be disturbing if the horizontal rather than the vertical diameter were smaller. In that case one could expect that the horizontal dimensions of the sun in its lower half would be most shortened, so that the sun would look like a pear with its stalk down. The impression of violence, implied in this configuration of the sun piercing through the horizon isn't appropriate to the setting sun. On the contrary, the impression created by it is that of reclining, without violence, without tension, of lingering on for a moment while already merging with the earth; this impression is like one of parting, which is right, for the day is over.

To this must be added that a horizontally contracted

sun, which would remain vertically large, would not only be large at the top because of the size of its vertical axis, but would also share in the heat and the blinding brilliance of the sun high in the sky. We would see an ambiguous sun, asking ourselves whether the day is really gone. But this sun which we see setting now leaves us with no doubts. This sun is totally an evening sun, from left to right and from top to bottom. Similarly, the rising sun is totally a morning sun, all over its shape, which increasingly becomes more detached from the earth and more tightly sketched.

Although this consideration is plausible in itself and sufficient to explain the concept of flattening, it doesn't really explain the fact that the sun is flattened on the horizon. This explanation, which is to be found in a different way, at first doesn"t seem to offer any difficulties. When the sun descends — I'll limit myself to the setting sun — it becomes larger. The dimension which doesn't keep up in this process of descending and becoming larger is, as always, the vertical one. For vertical dimensions become shorter when an object descends, in accordance with the first rule of dimensions that an object placed in a vertical position becomes larger in this direction. To this extent it is clear that the sun shows a flattening on the horizon.

Difficulties arise, however, when I include, as is required, the fourth rule of dimensions in my considerations. According to this rule, the process of the enlargement of things is more powerful, because of their closer proximity, than is the process of the shortening of vertical dimensions. In my first reflection I assumed that there are no exceptions to the fourth rule. But in that case the sun wouldn't be flattened but pearshaped and with the smaller part at the bottom. Does this mean that the fourth rule has only a restricted validity? Let us recall the example which led to the formulation of the rule, viz., the case of the weathercock. On the square at the bottom of the tower the cock was larger, in accordance with the third rule. And, again in accordance with this rule, the dimension from crest to feet was even greater. But this last point apparently doesn't apply to the sun. Why?

It makes no difference whether I put the weathercock upright on the square or leave it lying on the pavement. Upright the cock becomes even taller, just as the square and the pencil in the preceding reflection. Now, there is no doubt that there is a big difference between the ways in which the fallen cock and the setting sun have come down; so let us look for a solution to our problem in this difference. The cock lies at my feet in the square, but the sun, although it is closer than when it stood high in the sky, is still very far away. Farther away than all the mountains which I ever saw in the distance. Viewed from a distance, mountains are lower than when observed from their base. I recall my disappointment and surprise when I saw Mount Blanc for the first time in the distance. Was the highest mountain of Western Europe no taller than that? But the closer I got to it, the higher Mount Blanc became.

When one stands near the base of it, it impresses us as very high but when anyone moves away from it, it loses its height. New York's skyscrapers are disappointingly low when seen from a great distance. This means that at a long range the fourth rule apparently doesn't apply. There must be a perimeter around the observer, a circle which cannot be accurately circumscribed because it depends on many factors and which isn't even a geometrically orbicular circle; within this boundary the fourth rule is valid, but outside it the first rule of dimensions governs the situation. For this reason the sun is flat. This is my explanation, and I don't know of any other.

I realize, of course, that my explanation is quite different from the usual one. The latter can be summarized as follows. To reach us, the sun's rays must pass through the earth's atmosphere. Because the lower layers of air have a greater density, the rays from the bottom of the sun are more strongly curved than the curved rays from the sun's upper side. Thus the sun as a whole seems to stand higher than it really is in the sky; moreover, the bottom of this sun which is perceived too high, appears even higher than the top. This gives rise to the elliptical sun which, according to this explanation, then, is but an optical illusion.

Omitting this matter of optical illusion, what must be said about this explanation? First of all, it leaves no room for the fittingness of the sun's flattening. The curving of light in the atmosphere doesn't possess within itself anything that can be called meaningful. The curving of light is a neutral fact, as are its refraction and so many other properties of light and other phenomena of nature. Such terms as meaningful and meaningless are insignificant within the framework of those properties and qualities. The effect produced by the curving of the light rays in their passage through the atmosphere could, in this context, have just as well consisted in a vertically elongated sun or one that is flattened down to a horizontal line. But we see a sun with a slight flattening, which fits in with the evening. This sun is right, but no other. Any other shape would fall short or be disturbing. Now, *in order to attain this shape appropriate to the evening, the rays curve through the atmosphere in those various degrees.*

The usual explanation can be accepted, save for its neutrality. The latter reduces to an insignificant detail the result with which the explanation finishes — viz., the flattening of the sun — and which evidently was the purpose of the explanation. So, the rays coming from different parts of the sun curve to different extents when they pass through the atmosphere. Fine, I agree, I find it even splendid, but why do they curve? Among other reasons, in order to make the sun on the horizon flat to such and such a degree. The result has been attained! However, the explanation could have been different.

The red color of the rising and the setting sun invites a similar observation. The usual explanation of that color is just as simple as that of the sun's flattened shape. Light — in the second structure — consists of component parts having different wave-lengths. The red component of visible light has the greatest wave-length, and the blue component has the smallest. (Indigo and violet need not be considered here.) When light strikes the molecules of the atmosphere, it is scattered, but the various components of light do not scatter equally. Short wave light scatters more than long wave light. Now, when white light passes through the atmosphere, proportionately more of the red component passes than the blue. For this reason the sky is blue, and the sun near the horizon is red.

The striking element of this explanation is again the neutrality of the terms. If one did not know beforehand what the explanation led up to, one would be very much worried. Imagine, for example, that not blue but red would be more scattered. As far as the explanation is concerned, this wouldn't make any difference. But the result would be saddening. All day long one would see a fiery red heaven and at dusk a blue sun. A moon which would rise deep-blue above the horizon, would set just as "sky-blue" behind it. But this isn't the way things are. The moon and the sun are red, and the sky is blue. In order to achieve this, red has the longer wave-length and blue the shorter, and the atmosphere with certain molecules has a particular effect. It is in this complex way that that result has been achieved.

Could the red of the sun and the blue of the sky have been achieved in a different way? Although I don't know of any other explanation, I don't consider that as an argument. The explanation through the dispersion of light rays with different wave-lengths was, at first, unknown to me and, to tell the truth, is still unknown to me. I know *about* this explanation; I learned it at school. But I cannot say that it is as well known to me as is my own explanation, in principle. I know the evening and the morning; I know the difference between high and low; I know the blue sky with its red sun; I know the colored object. I am not as familiar with light. I know about them by way of a faultless argument. Similar faultless arguments made me accept wave-lengths and their differences in dispersion. But do I know them? I have to accept facts, but the facts could have been different. In that case another argument would have convinced me. Any other explanation would, in principle, have been just as valuable.

The chain of thought followed here leads me to a different evaluation of disturbing factors in the world around us which in other respects is meaningful. Let us begin with an example beyond the realm of colors. Light propagates itself more quickly than sound; or rather, because the velocity of propagating light in the above-mentioned sense isn't known to me, sound needs time to reach us, but not light. This is known to anyone who has ever seen and heard a woodcutter at work on the other side of a valley. First there is the visible stroke, which undoubtedly is synchronous with the action of the woodcutter, and then follows the audible sound. The difference in time measures the distance to the woodcutter. He visibly and audibly drives his axe into the wood at a certain distance.

The time differential, moreover, emphasizes the character of materiality of the intervening air. This materiality, of course, doesn't manifest itself only in this way but also in many others, by breathing, by running fast, by walking in the wind or by shaking a dust-rag. But seeing and hearing a woodcutter reveals a property of that materiality which hardly manifests itself if at all in the other examples. In the form of wind, air is material as resistance; the air which one inhales is material in the sense of breath, volume. But the air between me and the woodcutter is primarily a medium, intermediary matter. There is air between things. While things lie in the midst of air, they occupy space. One object lies farther away than another.

This point is readily evident from the fact that we look with both eyes, not with one. But this doesn't mean that we have two eyes mainly to be able to perceive depth, for winking to someone is important, and this is possible only for one who has two eyes. The same point, however, is also evident in a different way when we see and hear the woodcutter. He is as far away from us as we can both see and hear him strike his blows. Similar time differentials, albeit usually on a smaller scale, throughout the day give us impressions of the various distances at which things happen. It is meaningful that sound need time to reach us.

Let us now take another example. Seated in a car with open windows, we pass a barrel organ, playing in the street. Even at a distance we recognize the tune, but as we come closer the tune becomes louder and louder. Let us assume that it is a tune which we like. But the moment we pass the organ, the entire tune suddenly drops a few octaves in a really disturbing way. If sound didn't need any time —

or very little of it — to reach us, this phenomenon would hardly exist, if at all. But in that case the meaningful proof of the distance between us and the woodcutter and the equally meaningful demonstration of air as a medium would also be non-existent. It isn't right to demand everything at once.

Moreover, it shouldn't be forgotten that the hearer himself in his open car contributed to the dissonance. One who merely walks by an organ isn't troubled by dissonance, and a cyclist hardly notices any. If it were possible to fly past the organ in an airplane, the dissonance would be grotesque. It would drop from a rendition that is much too fast and impossibly high-pitched to one with the tempo and the intonation of the saddest funeral march. Of course, one cannot fly past a street organ; and even if it were possible, the plane's noise would prevent us from hearing the more subtle sounds of the organ.

Even in a motorcar this factor plays a role. The purring of the engine and the swishing of the air along the body of the car camouflage the falsety of the melody, so that we notice it only partially. Even a cyclist carries along a sound of his own. But the pedestrian is unhampered and doesn't hear a false tune. The dissonant element caused by the fact that sound needs time — a fact that in other respects is meaningful — enters this example only if one uses instruments of locomotion. The more these instruments embody knowledge derived from the second structure, the more one is troubled by the lowering of the tones; and this lowering finds its explanation in the second structure. Sound is propagated in waves; one who goes against the waves increases the frequency of those waves; hence he hears a higher sound, etc.

Not all disturbing phenomena, however, are the result of our own actions. An example is provided by the green ray at sunset. This example brings us back to the realm of colors. On a rare occasion, a small emerald-green flame sometimes appears after a clear sunset in the same place where the sun has set. The phenomenon lasts only a few seconds; its brief duration and its rarity account for the fact that few people know about it. The phenomenon might just as well not happen at all; no one, at any rate, would miss it. The green flame is superflous, and this impression is confirmed when one finally manages to see it: a tiny green ray of light which disappears in a flash. Why such a ray?

Much easier to answer is the question as to how that ray can be explained. This explanation is as follows. Under special atmospheric conditions it happens that, after sunset, a small bundle of light rays with the strongest refraction — the blue and green rays — can still reach the observer. These rays curve as it were around the globe, but this effect depends on so many rare factors that the effect of the green ray seldom occurs and even then lasts only a very short time. This, in a few words, is the explanation.

These few words, however, contain much. The phenomenon of the green ray wouldn't occur if the layer of air were thicker. Then, to name just one effect, the sun would give less heat to the earth, with all the consequences this implies. The green ray wouldn't occur if the earth were much larger, for the curvature of the earth wouldn't be big enough. But then the pull of gravity would be much greater; we would have much trouble moving around and precipitation would perhaps descent with so much force that all life would be disturbed. The phenomenon wouldn't exist if the earth didn't turn, for then the sun wouldn't set. The earth then would be baked by the sun on one side, while the opposite side would be very cold, with all of the water

stored there in the form of ice, and all the consequences
this then implies, and so on, for the enumeration is far from
complete.

So many conditions have to be fulfilled. If one keeps this
in mind, then the green ray — that tiny and unimportant
disturbance — is one that demands our respect. Let us add
a final example showing that "disturbing factors" should
be given their due value.

Water is heaviest at a temperature of four centigrades.
This property, to be heaviest at a temperature above the
freezing point, is found only in water and ammonia. It is
a rare but extremely important property. If liquid water
were heaviest at the freezing point, then water in a barrel
would freeze first at the bottom. And outside, first, for
example, on the bottom of the sea. In the winter, starting
from the poles, the sea would freeze from the bottom up.
It is improbable, even to be excluded, that the summer sun
could melt all the accumulated ice. Because of its low
density, the upper layer of warm or even hot water would
simply float over the underlying and increasingly cooler
layers, leaving the ice intact. Every winter the layer of ice
would increase, so that one can almost certainly say that
every sea, even in the tropics, would become one compact
mass of ice, over which would float a thin layer of warm
water in the summer and in the tropics a layer of very hot
water.

In this way everything on earth would be disrupted, and
life would hardly be possible. For whatever lives on earth
lives by the grace of an enormous quantity of water which
is stable in many of its properties. Even if the preceding
enumeration, which again is incomplete, contains erroneous
expectations, this single rare property — that water is heaviest above the freezing point — heralds a host of favorable

circumstances which must be fulfilled if the earth is to be able to support vegetative, animal and human life. This consequence can hardly be called insignificant.

For this property also there is an explanation in terms of the "second structure." It is as follows. Water is composed of oxygen and hydrogen. Every molecule possesses one atom of oxygen, connected with two atoms of hydrogen located at an angle of 108 degrees from each other. If the angle were 180° instead of 108°, as one would have expected, the property of highest density above the freezing point wouldn't have occurred, with all the consequences this entails. The angle that actually exists causes the water molecule to have two electric poles; and these, in their turn, produce the effect that the water molecules, when cooled, position themselves head to tail. It is this positioning which, by cooling below four centigrades, causes an ever increasing free space between the molecules, so that water, after continually shrinking in volume when cooled to four centigrades, begins again to occupy more space below that temperature. For the same reason ice occupies even more space, and this second rare property leads to other favorable consequences.

A splendid explanation! Any other commentary would be out of place. By means of this one peculiar property, "blind" as it is in itself, the masterpiece has been accomplished, for the sea doesn't freeze into one giant mass of ice, with all the consequences thereof, and the acids and salts in water ionize, with all the numerous useful and necessary consequences thereof. No one, then, should complain too much if his water pipes are cracked by frost, an effect that also follows from that meaningful condition, that peculiarity of water. It is a defect, of course, albeit one that lies within the realm of the strictly human existence; but this is a matter which offers no apology after all these considerations here. Besides, this same consequence causes rocks to be split by frost, so that in temperate zones more clay is formed than would otherwise have been the case. This, again, is a fact having numerous consequences. Nevertheless, it is a defect, one that compels respect. Only this defect? There might have been ten or twenty or more.

The green ray was a defect, but the masterpiece has been accomplished: a blue sky, a red setting sun; the entire panorama of colors which displays itself before our eyes in endless variations every day.

I can see that panorama here before me in one of those innumerable variations, one which can be found only in this spot on earth. The threat of the cumuli clouds above me has disappeared; they have been replaced by a fan of feathery streaks in a sky that is again transparent. Yet the sun has not yet entirely lost its yellowness. Far away, far beyond the fringe of trees around the meadow, it must have rained. There may have been a thunderstorm.

Why am I mentioning all these things? Only to show that the totality of the facts finds expression in every detail of the scenery. The grass here proves this special "moment." The same is done by the flowers, *at this moment,* but in their own way. Even the baluster, which lies on the grass as a mistake, shares in this moment. Everything constitutes this one whole, an all-encompassing totality of glory in many ways. It doesn't take any effort to accept the fact that many components were needed to achieve this whole. It would be wrong on my part if I didn't appreciate these factors at their true value.

THE SHAPE OF THE EARTH AND ARCHITECTURE

Chapter Three

Here comes my friend. "How can you stand it?" he exclaims. He is right, for I am now sitting out in the sun. But he doesn't know what I've seen and reflected upon here. My position was ideal for reflection. If one wishes to study light and colors, he must not shield himself from the sun. Could one see the desert from an air-conditioned room? As little, I think, as one could see the qualities of this scenery from a laboratory.

"You took a long nap," I tell my friend. "Were you tired?" He doesn't answer. He stretches his arms, yawns, collapses into a chair and sighs: "A pity that we've left our wives at home." Even before he has finished his sentence, a slight, weak, unexpected, but familiar change occurs in the scenery. The change is almost too ephemeral to seize and hold with the eye. Or am I perhaps mistaken? Is anything really changed? I am somewhat skeptical about things changing. But today I want to see real things about which no one ever told me that they could be seen. I see it, I saw it and I still see it: the reality of the grass, the flowers and the trees became different, a little softer, as a faint gloaming fell over them. In a moment another world announced itself, a lovely world of nature, in which time hardly moved. This was a somewhat evanescent world. A little more of this and my afternoon reflections would be over.

"Let us look at the facade again," says my friend. We go down the steps, walk across the grass and look at the house. "You see," he says, "now we are getting somewhere." "Broader balusters," he adds, "would have overaccentuated the porch. Then the facade, which on the whole isn't bad, would have been less imposing. Thin balusters wouldn't have done enough for the facade, and the porch would have looked somewhat clumsy. The card-board balusters made the facade too high. But things are okay now. This nice porch is going to give the house its proper proportions." I see that he is right.

However, I have to be cautious in my observation. If I observe the house at one glance, my friend is right; it is becoming a well-proportioned house. But this initial and apparently justified impression disappears when I try to look at it more carefully, considering each detail of the house and trying to measure them with my eye. "That impression disappears," I said, but it doesn't really. The initial impression just becomes less valid, less plausible. In fact, that first impression might be considered somewhat rash. What exactly does it mean that the porch influences the facade?

I cannot get rid of the question. Does the facade ultimately remain the same or not? The same doubt which I thought that I had overcome keeps recurring. Habit plays tricks with me, the habit of a centuries-old tradition. I have been taught to call the change mere appearance. I have no certainty in the matter. At any rate, the first impression returns whenever I look at the facade; besides, my first impression isn't dependent on the duration of my glance. I thought so a moment ago; certainly the first impression is clearest at the moment when I begin to see. Yet I can maintain that impression; all I have to do is avoid isolating details and wishing to measure them. As long as I observe this rule, which goes against the habit which we all received from tradition, I can prolong the first impression to any point I wish. In this way my conviction that the facade changes remains. But what is this conviction?

"You are kind of quiet," my friend remarks, "don't you agree with me?" "That's not it," I reply, "but I wonder what I am seeing; reality or an optical illusion?" I tell him about my doubt. "If one could put the facade on the ground," I say in order to provoke him, "the impression would vanish." My friend is a sober man. "Put the facade on the ground?" he says, "that would leave me without a summer home! And what an optical illusion that would then be! Illusion pure and simple." The idea amuses him. "Imagine" he adds, "that I would then open the door in that facade. What would I see? Nothing but a wrecked lawn. I will prove to you that there is something else. You must be dying of thirst. Shall we drink something? A cool drink will be good for us." "Okay," I answer, "you get it, while I keep worrying. Nothing strong, please."

I know what alcohol can do. In a short time the entire panorama would change. I have seen fields vibrate and undulate. It can be delicious though, necessary even. There are sceneries which disclose their true character only after a few glasses of wine. It can be a delight, but it isn't what I want right now while I am trying to understand mysteries of a different nature.

Meanwhile my friend has disappeared through the door

of his vertical facade. That term, facade, is deceptive; too much connected with the horizontal blueprint. What I see is a house, a house with rooms. Although I cannot see the rooms in the ordinary, visual, sensory sense of the term, nevertheless, I perceive them. These are rooms in which my friend is visible here or there, even though I don't see him now. Again there is a difference here between seeing and seeing. Now I see my friend appear on the porch in a directly visible way. He throws his hands up in despair. "Sorry," he says, "but we'll have to practice patience. The fuse is blown and I have no spares here. I'll go and buy one. Meanwhile try not to die of thirst."

I lie down on the grass. How this house intrigues me! Now that I lie stretched out on my right side, nothing can be said about the dimensions. Are they high, low, broad, narrow? In my position one eye is vertically above the other, and now these questions don't make sense. Even the depth of the house has vanished. Yes, now I see a facade. What is the house without my impression? I assume a sitting position; now I see again a house. Before I realize it, I've already started my third reflection.

Third Reflection

Those balusters are beginning to annoy me. Let me summarize the facts again. I wish to know what it is that I see. If the balusters taper in an upward direction, the facade becomes wide; if they taper in a downward direction, it becomes high. Broad balusters don't do justice to the facade; narrow balusters won't allow the facade to be significant. Which balusters will let the house be "itself"? Those which influence it least, the narrow ones. But even these exercise some influence on the porch. They would make the porch, as

my friend said, appear somewhat clumsy; and I am sure too
that a clumsy-looking porch would directly affect the house.
The house would "say very little" and would itself also be
clumsy. So we shouldn't use narrow balusters. But, then
what kind of balusters should we use? If this house is to
be "itself," that is, be such that no one, with the best will
in the world, can still speak of an illusion, then every influence that the balusters have on the house will have to
disappear.

This goal can only be reached if the porch has no balusters at all. All right, then, no balusters, a porch without
any balusters. But even a porch without them does something to the facade. So we will also have to get rid of the
porch. But now the lid is off. For what I've said of the balusters and the porch can be repeated for every part of the
house; for instance, the windows. What kind of windows
let the house be "itself"? Narrow windows? Broad windows?
High, low, large, small windows? So, no windows at all if
the house is to be this one, concrete house. No windows,
no doors, no gutters, no roof. No facade at all would be
the best solution, for even a facade without windows, doors
and gutters influences the house. No rooms either, and no
foundation. And thus I am led to conclude that the house
is "itself" if it doesn't exist.

An interesting conclusion. If I ask what shape, size and
dimensions any attribute of the house must have in order
to let the house be "this house" uninfluenced by anything,
I arrive at the conclusion that that attribute can best be left
out enirely. My question must be wrong. I shouldn't ask
when this house will be "itself." I don't even know what is
meant by the "self" of the house.

Meaningful is the question, How is this house here and
now? Then I can answer: with this kind of baluster it is

high, with that kind low. Does one kind have preference? Yes, of course; that's why we are bestowing so much care on the house. But this preference isn't concerned with the character of reality of this house. True, that preference rules over there, over the house, rather than over us; to this extent this preference is real, for it belongs to the domain of reality. But with or without this or that preference the house exists anyhow. The house is just as real with any kind of porch. With narrow or broad balusters, with round or angular ones, with balusters that taper in this or that direction. The house is always there, full of reality. Otherwise I am indulging in reflections which eliminate the house.

I now understand my uneasiness when I visited the St. Peter's in Rome and asked myself about the usual explanation concerning the influence which the two squares in front of the church exercise on the large ornamented facade. Anyone who visits Rome is told about it. When the church was finished, a lack of proportion revealed itself in the facade, and this defect was caused by the intricate history of its building. This intricacy resulted from one of the greatest revolutions in architectural styles the West has ever known. At first, the plans for St. Peter's didn't call for a nave, but the originally conceived edifice was to have a foundation shaped like a regular octagon. Later, when different ideas prevailed about the nature and function of a church, the nave was added. This addition had a disastrous influence on the giant cupola above the octagon; moreover, it led to that colossal facade which was much too large and squat. To remove the last-named disturbing impression, two ingeniously conceived squares were added in front of the facade. In front of it they built the so-called rectangular square, which on a plan is actually shaped like a trapezium;

and before this "rectangular" square lies the so-called "round" square, which on the plan is actually oval or elliptical.

But one who enters these squares finds them really square and round, and it is precisely for this reason that they can exercise their peculiar influence on the facade. The first, seemingly rectangular but trapezium-shaped square makes the facade just as broad as the short side of the trapezium which is most distant from the facade is long; at the same time, the oval square, because it is seen as a circle, places the facade at a greater distance. Even more artifices were used, which together produce the desired effect of making the facade lose its broad and squat appearance. That effect has been achieved.

What is it that has been achieved here? The usual explanation is: an artful whole, based on an optical illusion. But an optical illusion normally and correctly means something else. One who in the forest thinks that a tree-stump is a pheasant is the victim of an optical illusion. One can recognize this illusion by clapping one's hands or by walking up to the stump and then seeing that it isn't a pheasant but a stump. In order to make this verification, one has to fulfill certain conditions — walking up to the stump and looking — but these conditions can be eliminated by returning to one's original position and there observing that the same illusion doesn't repeat itself. One can then say: what I see resembles a pheasant but it is a tree-stump. Most of the time one will wonder how one could ever have been so careless.

An optical illusion is a mistake in perception; often it is a meaningful mistake. It makes sense, for example, that a person who is afraid in the forest has many illusory perceptions in line with his fear — which is a property of *his* forest.

But one who does not suffer from that fear — from *that* kind of forest — and has the same illusions makes mistakes. He is willing, of course, to recognize his mistakes, whereas the man filled with fear is much less inclined to do. Moreover, one's optical illusions occur more frequently when one is alone than in company with others. A person who is full of fear is alone even when he is with others. He has the woods to himself. Thus I conclude that an illusion consists in an erroneous perception; this error is rarely made by many at the same time; usually only a few, and then mostly people who are alone, make it.

The perception of St. Peter's facade is an entirely different matter. First of all, everyone shares in it; and in this respect the situation is similar to that of the tower mentioned before. Not just one or two people, but everyone at the foot of the tower sees that it is higher than it appears to be when it is staked out on a horizontal plane. A similar remark applies to the baluster out there on the lawn, near the flowers. From the porch everyone sees that baluster as being longer.

Secondly, the verification which eliminates an illusion is powerless with respect to St. Peter's. No matter how often one stands before the facade and observes that it is heavy and broad, one can also see, if standing back at the beginning of the round square, that it isn't too bad. If one didn't know from his travel guide that the facade without the squares is broad and squat even at a distance, one could ask oneself where the optical illusion is supposed to begin. In the case of a true optical illusion this would not be possible, or only rarely in more or less artificial situations. The same holds true for the tower. Knowing the length of the tower in feet, one can lay out this distance horizontally at the foot of the tower and then say: the tower is this high.

But that statement is not convincing. Looking up, one exclaims: I can't believe it.

It is indeed incredible; and there is no need to force oneself to believe it. The bricks of the tower stretch and shrink according to the direction in which they are set. Is such a connection also applicable to St. Peter's? It is, I think. Viewed over the two squares, the facade is narrower. This effect is caused by these squares; there is no doubt about it. If the squares before the church were removed, the facade would be broader. But what would there be in place of the two squares? Houses? But houses also exercise influence. A bare open space? But then the facade would undoubtedly be even broader and heavier than one sees it now from nearby. Regardless of what stands before St. Peter's, it always exercises influence on the facade. To obtain an unaffected facade, one would have to tear it down. In order to eliminate all influence, one has to use the greatest of all influences, that of destruction. There is always an influence; and this term is beginning to please me less and less. There is always another St. Peter's, and none of these is more real than the others. This is the same conclusion which I had already reached before in a different context.

Another illustration comes to my mind here, one on a smaller scale. This is related to the baluster which I threw out on the lawn and which lies now beside me. Much attention has been paid in psychology to the following experiment. Two lines of equal length are drawn on a piece of paper. Next, arrow heads are drawn at both ends of the two lines, with this difference that on the first line the arrows are open toward the ends of the line and on the second line they are open away from the ends. The first line now looks much shorter than the second, although they were of equal length and therefore will have remained equal in length.

That, at least, is the usual explanation, which has made this experiment famous as a beautiful and simple proof of optical illusion. This term, however, again gives rise to objections. First of all, everyone, regardless of the conditions, will always see two different lengths. Secondly, one doesn't become convinced when, using a ruler, one observes that the two lines are equal. One knew this beforehand because the procedure is familiar. One sees, and continues to see, two different lengths, even after the verification. Besides, what makes the qualification "optical illusion" objectionable is this: why should the two "bare" lines enjoy any priority? Are they more real than the two "dressed" lines? The former can be measured with a ruler, the latter evidently not. One is surprised to observe that these two "dressed" lines are of equal length beside the ruler. Are they of equal length? There should be no surprise about the unexpected equality of length, for they remain visibly unequal, but there should be some surprise about the ruler which, so it appears, stretches and shrinks with the lines it measures.

Strictly speaking, this phenomenon need not surprise us either. The ruler itself is a "bare" line, even the prototype of such a line. If the ruler is placed in different contexts — for example, placed perpendicularly, or provided with arrow heads at the end as in the psychological experiment — then it also assumes different dimensions, the numbers marking the centimeters notwithstanding. A length without context is least real and the poorest of all lengths. Besides — let me repeat it — the poverty of this length itself is also a context, that of a "bare" line with nothing around it. Bareness and emptiness are the conditions on which lines are equal, so that this equality is always artificial and forced.

There is no equality anywhere in the things around us. Thus, is it justifiable to deny inequality with an appeal to that artificial and forced equality? The answer to this question is a new argument against the opinion that an optical illusion is involved in the experiment with the two lines.

My thoughts return to St. Peter's. Walking up the round square with the colonnades, I am delighted with the facade which was once too large and squat before the two squares were added. It has become narrower because of them. This sentence should be understood literally. The stones of the facade have shrunk in breadth through the building of the two squares. From where I stand, at the beginning of the round square, I see stones that have diminished in breadth. If I still doubt this, I can perform the following experiment — one which I have often made, and always with the same result, which is the hallmark of a good and successful experiment.

I walk across the two squares toward the facade. First the round square; when I reached the end of it, the facade begins already to increase in breadth. Then the rectangular square; now that I stand close to the facade, I am overpowered by it. Such an enormous facade! It is broad; it has become so much broader that it is difficult for me to identify this broad facade with the much smaller structure I saw at first. It looks like one different from the first facade, yet related to it. Next, I retrace my steps across the two squares to my original starting point, stopping from time to time and turning around. At each turn the facade is smaller. I see the stones diminish in size, just as I saw them expand when I walked in the opposite direction.

Any other description wouldn't do justice to what I perceive; that is to say, it wouldn't do justice to the facade. What is at stake is not my perception but the facade.

For what is a facade if it isn't seen? The facade has been built to be seen. This means that the eyes are at stake, and so is my perception, but now not as something incidental, much less as a disturbing element. All things are themselves perceived things. Perception belongs to things as something that is inalienable to them.

When I stood close to the facade, it was enormous; its breadth was part and parcel of its vastness. When I walked back, the facade became less enormous and also less broad. My walk produces not only a change in breadth, but also and especially a change in character. The latter change implies the former, and it is at the same time the proper change that occurred. The change in character contains the change in breadth. From the change in character I can abstract that in breadth. I realize, however, that for reasons which we have already considered, I should be careful in this matter. This is why I often repeated my walk across the squares: I wished to see exactly what happened to the facade as a whole and, at the same time, to notice exactly how in this totality breadth, as a separate factor, increased and decreased. Well, the breadth of the facade changed in the way described above. This gave me confidence that my abstraction had not gone too far. Much more happened than this change, however; this was certain. Let me therefore proceed to a new abstraction, one that has more substance than that of breadth.

I stand on the round square with the collonades and look at St. Peter's. What do I see? That depends on the time, the company I am with and numerous other factors. But I want to be abstract. What do I see effortlessly when I am alone? A church, and its architecture. Thousands of others have seen that before me, of course. I see a cupola which unfortunately is well-hidden. A facade, columns, steps; a picture with which I am very familiar, though this is a poor way of expressing it. I see an Italian sky, tourists, clerical garbs, people, gestures. There are people everywhere going in different directions in a way that pleases the eye. Behind them, the facade, that architecture. This is what I wish to keep in mind as I cross the squares and approach the facade.

At first the facade remains a piece of architecture. But as I ascend the broad steps on the second square, the facade becomes enormous. It fascinates me. Now as I stand directly in front of it, it almost overpowers me. This wall, this facade with all its history. This entrance to another world. This is what I realize standing before these towering columns: a different world announces itself here. This is an impression which even the most inveterate humanist cannot escape. I don't want to enter the church yet, for I know from experience that it will be much too confusing at first, a tumult of shapes and lines which will become orderly only after frequent visits and many discussions of what one sees and reads about them.

Every church is a challenge, and especially this one. I therefore wish to stay in front of the facade a little longer, and meet the challenge there. People pass me going in and out of the church. Some people look up at the stones in amazement. But I also see others, who are used to it, look at nothing and enter the portals as if there were no threshold. All of these people are on a boundary, out here or in there. Some remain outside even when they go inside. Others take the inside with them when they go outside; the church goes beyond the steps, to the two squares and deep into the outside world from which I have come. The facade is all movement, it is a moving, yielding boundary which remains self-consistent. A wall which relocates its power.

"Well," I say to myself, "let me touch this wall, feel the stone which accomplished this feat." I feel hard material, stone, earth, rock. Of course. Nevertheless, I don't feel the rock of the rocky landscape from which the stone was cut. If I wished, I could undoubtedly feel that same rock, but then I would almost commit a crime. My gesture would then move the stone back to the place of its origin. That wouldn't be right, for the stone has been brought here for a reason. If the stone wasn't meant to be changed, it could have been left where it was. It was given a function, an additional property. Gradually this function merged with the stone. Generations learned to use the stone, it assumed a place in our history. The multitudes who entered and left through this facade, whether alone, in groups, in processions, in silence, talking or singing, laughing or crying, these multitudes gave the stone its character, its substance.

It is a new substance which I can feel with the palm of my hand. I would feel even better if I wore a cassock that could slide along the stones. (of course, I don't wear a cassock.) I must be careful with my hands. To put a hand on the stones, that's all right, but to scratch them with my nails wouldn't be right. That would go counter to the function of the stone, my scratches would damage its substance. One doesn't scratch portals, at least not the portal of this boundary. That's why no one is tempted to do this. I have never seen anyone merely lay the palm of his hand against the stones, although this would be the slightest form of touch. Thousands, even tens of thousands pass through this facade on a single day, yet no one touches the stones and certainly no one scratches them with his nails. But if those crowds were led through the quarry where the stones were cut, many of them would then pick up a piece and test it with their nails to see how hard the stone is.

There such an action would be right, but here at the facade the stone's being does not permit that.

As I recall walking again on those two squares, my memory unites my impressions into a single picture. My respect for those who planned and build the complex known as "St. Peter's" becomes much greater, despite all the bad things which have been said and written about it, with some justification. The cupola, the nave, the facade, the two squares with their unique shapes and typical circumscription. A revolution in architecture, and especially in men's style of life, is solidified in the complex. Not a stone in it is out of place. Such an integrity — which need not be synonymous with beauty — can be found in virtually all edifices that were planned by a master and which, through generations of use, have become the common possession of all. One finds it in the San Lorenzo basilica, the churches of Vezelay and Sens, the Santa Maria della Consolazione in Todi, the Gesù of Rome, the town square of Salamanca, and the Neue Wache of Berlin.

I realize that the past generations have attached to them a tradition of use and appreciation and that I look at them in these terms. But it would be wrong on my part to think that that tradition operates in me only as a transferred opinion which has nothing to do with those edifices as such. I learn to distinguish that tradition in the stone. By means of conversation about and reflection upon such an edifice, and by frequent visits to it, I learn to know the stone. This is my experience; and I know that many others share it. Gradually the stone becomes familiar, and then one's admiration increases for the giants who dared to build these structures. Imagine. In the stone quarry there is nothing but rock, pieces of rock, shapeless matter, recalcitrant earth. The builder has to start with this earth, no matter how much thinking and sketching he does beforehand. He begins with a poor and lifeless substance, with the intention of overcoming this lifelessness step by step. And he does this first and foremost by measuring.

To measure is to make it horizontal or to keep it horizontal if nothing has as yet been erected. All the planning involved in construction such edifices are first completed by the architect on his blueprint, which is a horizontal plane. Similarly the transportation of stones from the quarry to the construction site and their arrival there happen on the horizontal plane. But the architect hopes to achieve vertically what he has designed horizontally. This is a work of art of the first magnitude. The rules which govern the transition from the horizontal plane to the vertical alter the dimensions.

For example, the architect who builds a church in Greek Ionic or Doric style will discover that both the right and the left side of the facade are too low if he sets out the dimensions horizontally on his blueprint without paying attention to the rules which govern the transition from the horizontal to the vertical. As a result the edifice seems then to bulge in the center. If the horizontal lines drawn on the paper are also to run horizontally in the vertical facade, then the architect must curve the lines on his paper. Other examples could be cited here, all of which show that the topic "horizontal-vertical" is a difficult chapter in architecture, one which the architect, moreover, must be able to handle with a certain flair.

An even greater masterpiece is visible when the edifice is finished. The house, which is a *house,* and the church, which is a *church,* don't come about automatically. The edifice has a function, a suitable function, one which can even sometimes strike us at once.

But the greatest masterpiece of all undoubtedly is seen when the edifice, through centuries of use, has assumed its true, carefully polished form, its character, its historical essence and when it has become, in the literal sense of the term, a monument, a memorial. It is only by scratching the surface that one can then discover the old stone in the new.

The new stone, moreover, is not at all stable. I got some proofs of it which I am not likely to forget. Once I was visiting St. Peter's, I leaned against one of the four enormous pillars which support the cupola in order to look up into this structure. I realize that the cupola was so high that the "Dom," the famous medieval church tower of Utrecht, could be placed under it. I could hardly believe it. Today I would simply say that it isn't believeable. The verticality of the Dom tower dates from a different era, making its caliber so different from that of St. Peter's interior that the tower cannot fit into it. The tower is taller. But at the time I merely asked myself how I could think of comparing the dimensions of a free-standing tower with those of a church built in such a different style, and especially with the internal dimensions of that church. As I was reflecting upon this matter, I kept gazing up, trying to realize what height is in a church. As I was doing this, I was unexpectedly distracted by the pleasant fragrance of perfume.

Its refined fragrance had reached my nose and made me carefully breathe more deeply. When such a fragrance reaches a man, his imagination goes to work. Moreover, anything can be expected in St. Peter's. Was a Swedish blonde standing next to me? Or perhaps a dark-haired Italian beauty? The perfume was a tiny bit too Spanish for that. Although I intentionally continued to gaze up, being partially motivated by discretion, my attention had suffered. What was I to do with that cupola now that this woman with her perfume was standing next to me? IIad she not captivated me by that fragrance? Breathing the same air as she, I could believe that. I felt like a man. Of course, I had been a man all the time I had been standing there. A man sees things differently from a woman, even at the many moments when he doesn't pay attention to his sex. Things are different for a man and for a woman; if they weren't how could they discover their sex?

From each other, as I can see at this moment. But this discovery would be poor and, in all probability, would quickly be limited to an animal level if the recognition remained restricted to that "from each other." True, a woman is bodily infinitely different for a man, just as the man also is bodily infinitely different for a woman. A woman's hands, her gaze, the voice and her more sexual features are astonishing. So is her hair. But a woman's hair is hair gently blown by a breeze, hair against a certain background. The eye of a woman sees objects and people; her voice speaks of things and people. The woman is a world for the man; that has been said often enough already.

But I doubt that it has been said with sufficient meaning. For when the perfume reached my nose in St. Peter's, a change occurred which affected everything I saw. I wasn't chased away from the cupola; instead a new cupola arose before my eyes. Vaguely a charm that was familiar but still neutral and uncommitted began to envelop the stone. It was a change much like the one I experienced a quarter of an hour ago. Everything changed before my eyes when my friend sighed because we had left our wives at home. Yet, the church retained its identity as a church, even as this particular monument, the same memorial of the past.

But, oh my! what a mistake I had made about the person standing beside me. I wanted to know who was there, so

I glanced over and saw not a woman but a man standing beside me. A priest. A short Contra-Reformation priest, neatly groomed, well-manicured and dressed in an immaculate lace surplice, stood at my side. *He* had permeated the air with that fragrance. All at once the fragrance had become different. The female element had vanished from it, and in its place was a sweetish kind of priesthood, an "odor of sanctity" of an inferior quality, related to those Sacred Heart pictures and images of very pinkish Madonnas. Obviously, the fragrance had not entirely lost its femininity.

I no longer wanted to inhale this fragrance, which had changed for me. I felt contaminated by it. At the same time, St. Peter's had changed. True, I still saw the same church, the same pillars, the same mosaics. But all at once this same church and all its contents belonged to a particular form of Christianity, a much too Roman form. It hurt my feelings to know that I stood there. A few moments ago I was enjoying the colors and forms, easily sharing in the faith that so visibly guarded the walls. Now I saw an ostentatious edifice from times past, one that had had its function. It had become a different kind of memorial in all its details.

That stone edifice of St. Peter's revealed still another meaning when, by way of a special favor, I was able to attend one of the morning sessions of Vatican Council Two. The nave of the church was occupied by bishops and cardinals in purple and red. On one of the balconies I could see the *periti,* and just ahead of me, close to the altar, the invited representatives of other churches. A colorful and diligent gathering, which gave a new aura to the old stone. The spectacle of this gathering erased the image of the little priest in his surplice. I can still hear the subdued sound of those many voices in the immense nave. I can still see and hear their loud buzzing in the coffeerooms. Could I assume that the stones in one of these coffeerooms remained the same after the priests dropped their cookie crumbs on them? It seemed just as easy for me to assume that the changed stones caused the priests to drop their crumbs. Drop them in full view of Calvinists, who also dropped crumbs over their suits. I enjoyed the sight. No one was annoyed by it, no one was surprised that the church tolerated this. The stone had changed.

When I enthusiastically told my friend about my experiences in Rome, he was afraid that I would become a Catholic. But that isn't the issue. It is, I think, no longer so much the issue for anyone, unless one seeks a particular destiny in a particular form of Christian faith, such as wishing to become a religious or wishing to have unity of faith in the family with one's future wife who is a Catholic. For this last-named reason one also becomes a Protestant. But the term "Protestant" has lost its vigor, just as much as the term "Roman Catholic." What was it, then, that led me to the Council?

In October, 1957, the first earth satellite was hurled into its orbit. In April, 1961, the first man orbited around the earth. Between these two dates, in January, 1959, the first announcement was made about the Council, which was solemnly opened on October 11, 1962. I don't think that there was any direct connection between space travel and Vatican Council II, but wasn't there an indirect connection? Could two such important revolutionary events happen at the same time and have no connection at all? History teaches us that simultaneous events of this magnitude are usually, if not always, connected.

If I am to stay within the context of the circumstances which led me to Rome, and follow the various stages of

Western religious convictions, then it isn't difficult to discover that each of those stages is at the same time an era marked by a special scientific insight or undertaking in the West. The parallelism is so great that, looking at the years of important events in one category, one can predict where in the other category its important events will be located; sometimes one can surmise — or even know for certain — what those events were.

Mysticism and mathematics, terms which are intentionally chosen, run parallel. I intend to write a book about this and the things connected with it, a book big enough to explain more clearly than I can do here the character of so-called matter. For both mysticism and mathematics are concerned with matter. This book will contain a "theory of the changes of matter." [1] The preparation of this work caused me to ask for permission to be present at some of the sessions of the Council. There, in St. Peter's, so loaded with the spirit of the Counter-Reformation, the same spirit which also marked the development of the physical sciences, should become evident what dominates these same sciences today now that that spirit is vanishing. Much became clear to me, but it will be very difficult to say exactly what I perceived, heard, discussed and reflected upon. That difficulty has already manifested itself here.

In their historical development mysticism and mathematics run parallel. Mysticism, properly understood, is the core of every faith. Mathematics, also properly understood, is the core of the physical sciences. These sciences are concerned with matter, and so is faith, but in an entirely different way. The difference can be briefly explained in this way. The space in which we breathe, live and strive, act

---

[1] This work was published in Dutch in 1969 under the title *Metabletica van de Materie,* Nijkerk, 1969. Ed.

and go our way, has two forms or shapes, which can be referred to as profane and sacred. Shape or form are vague, provisional terms. In any true church one becomes familiar with sacred space, and from this church that space extends itself throughout the world with the exception of a few sparse places. Profane space also permeates all places. One can prove this by scratching matter with one's nails, for this can be done anywhere in the world.

It is possible to think and act scientifically in a church. It is even possible to build a laboratory in it, but inevitably the sacred space which is proper to the church would vanish. With a few exceptions, it is also possible to live anywhere in the world in a church, that is, in the community of faith. One can even build a church almost anywhere. This visible church, this edifice is, likewise, the visible manifestation of the difference between sacred and profane space. To experience this, one has only to enter a church.

With respect to this elementary experience, the style of that church is irrelevant. Whether one enters a basilica dating from before the year 1000, a Romanesque or Gothic cathedral, a Renaissance church or a Baroque church, one is always struck by the same transition in spite of all the differences. There is the same "halt" and the same invitation. Even a nineteenth century church — an epoch which didn't have a style of its own and which at the same time, was characterized by a brazen scientific optimism — exhibits the same threshold. The threshold manifests itself with a new luster in today's churches. One has only to look at the portals of any church to realize that things are different inside and outside. The portals, the facade, the walls of the church and roof together constitute one visible boundary between two spaces.

Let me give an example. Around 1740 writings appeared,

together with other evidence, proving that the Baroque era had passed. The Baroque style had begun around 1540, lasting about two centuries. A Neogothic and Neoclassical period began after 1740 and lasted till the twentieth century. These names demonstrate that this period was lacking in a style of its own. It is now rightly described as the most barren era of church architecture. This evaluation must not be seen in isolation from the whole of church life. For if the church is unable to have a contemporary style of its own in an era, what is one to think of the faith which guides the church during that period? Theologians also agree that the period from about 1740 to the twentieth century has been, so far as the life of faith is concerned, an impoverished era with too much emphasis on the interiority of man's subjectivity.

Oft-quoted examples of this are eighteenth century pietism and the theology of sentiment which flowed from it and dominated the nineteenth century. A faith based on an individual's sentiments is, as a faith without an object, a faith without a space of its own. This immediately throws light on the fact that this era did not produce any church style of its own. If a faith doesn't have a space of its own, then the lack of a concrete sacred world which follows from this deficiency, makes it impossible for that faith to set a boundary for that world.

At this point it is important to see what has happened in the profane world since 1740. First of all, let us indicate what the end of the Baroque style signified. Surveying the different Western styles before Baroque, such as the Basilica, the Romanesque style, the Gothic style and the Renaissance style one can say that the styles which followed the Basilica were one sustained and initially almost desperate attempt to preserve the original sacred space given in the Basilica. Each of these styles failed, especially because of the exaggerated tendency to strive for height; yet each time it seemed possible to find a new form appropriate to the time. For the life of faith this meant that each time room was found in which the old faith could be relocated. But after 1740 it no longer appeared possible to do this.

In principle the same must apply to profane space. Until about 1740 there was still room in which the old established certainties could be preserved. But after 1740 this must become impossible. This means, literally, that after 1740 the space in which these certainties had been valid for centuries had to be devalued or even to perish entirely. Now, one important certainty of space prior to 1740 is a proposition that is fundamental for mathematics and for everything connected with mathematics, viz., the proposition that the sum of the angles of a triangle is equal to a straight angle. It is then to be expected that the certainty expressed in this proposition, so fundamental for profane space, will find it very difficult to find room in the space dating from around 1740. As a matter of fact, we find that in 1733 the first writing appeared which manifested with some hesitation a non-Euclidean doubt; and with the beginning of the theology of sentiment a first audacious attempt was made to investigate the theory that the sum of the angles of a triangle is really equal to that of a straight angle. In past centuries no one had ever tried this. Yet, nothing else was to be expected. On this side of the Neogothic or Neoclassicist wall non-Euclidean space is tantamount to sentimental pietism which is on the other side of that wall.

My friend is late. So I may as well pursue my theme. My thoughts continue to roam through the days of the past which underlie our way of living and thinking. To the extent that it is possible here, I'd like to arrange my thoughts in an orderly fashion concerning the synchronism of both spaces and about the church as a visible manifestation of what happens in both spaces. Let me begin with the oldest period of Christianity in the West, the period which, so far as church style is concerned, is dominated by the Basilica.

The Basilica has straight, level walls, supporting a simple saddle roof. Because of the effortless balance achieved by this simple style, the Basilica doesn't need additional supports such as arches. The church has an elongated nave, usually divided in three or five sections and separated by columns. The simplicity which characterizes the space of the Basilica is connected with the lengthy shape of the church, the level interior ceiling and the absence of any attempt at achieving height. But all styles following the Basilica were marked by this striving for height and experienced its recalcitrance. This tendency soon manifested itself in the Romanesque style, which succeeded the Basilica from about the year 1000. At the same time, simplicity disappeared. This disappearance can be seen in the turbulent ornamentation of the capitals and especially in the arches of the roof. A visitor to the Romanesque church of Vezelay who looks up into the central nave feels as though the bricks of the arches will come tumbling down at any moment. The feeling of unrest continues in the elongated nave, which, to our relief, is supported on the outside with buttresses.

The Gothic style came next; it began around 1130 and continued till the middle of the fifteenth century. Height was the supreme goal in this style. Its various characteristics — the pointed arch, the ribs of the vault, the supporting flying buttresses outside, and the exceptionally large, non-supporting windows — are all designed for one purpose, to achieve height. And it was this height which caused the style to die out. The cathedral of Beauvais illustrates this point. This church was intended to be the highest of all Gothic cathedrals, but it collapsed, unfinished after two centuries of building and was never rebuilt. But the sanctuary and the two transepts have been spared, so that one can still see what an overwhelming desire for height the church had to satisfy. Both the Romanesque and the Gothic style died out from height.

The next style was that of the Renaissance. It lasted only a short time in the building of churches, undoubtedly because the sacred space necessary for the Christian faith could not be realized in the Renaissance church. But there was nothing else at the time. The dream of height had passed in failure. What remained possible was the expression of this failure. For this the pagan temple offered the example. No matter how high the church would be, there would be no nave, no height. St. Peter's cupola shows this: it isn't high, even though travel guides say that the famous Dom tower of Utrecht can stand under it with room to spare. The Sainte Chapelle of Paris is higher. On the other hand, there was simplicity in the Renaissance church, but this simplicity was unlike that of the Basilica. It was essentially a round, closed temple, suggesting that the smallest possible ground surface and the smallest possible sacred space had to be sufficient.

Around 1540 the Baroque style began. The Renaissance-like temple continued in the Baroque church, but a long nave was added to it. The Gesù in Rome is a splendid example of this style, one which, as a matter of fact, served as a model for innumerable churches. The church has a new and imposing long nave, but the flat surface of the facade characterizes the Renaissance-like temple. Thus the Baroque church is a compromise of the original, simple sacred space, which was uncomplicated by the attempt at achieving height, and the sacred space that had been violated by this attempt. The Baroque style lasted for two centuries.

Around 1740 Neoclassic and Neogothic styles arose. They were almost complete opposites, yet neither was able to create a sacred space proper to that time. People were satisfied with copying and continued to do this until about 1900. The twentieth century, however, again enjoys the privilege of a genuine sacred space of its own.

To summarize this brief survey, the styles and their times are as follows:
Basilica, until 1000
Romanesque style, 1000-1130
Gothic style, 1130-1450
Renaissance style, 1450-1540 (but the typically high-Renaissance style of church building covers only the last four decades of the period 1450-1540)
Baroque style, 1540-1740
Neogothic and Neoclassical styles, 1740-1900
Twentieth century style, since 1900.

The sequence of the various style changes is as follows:
uncomplicated long nave without an attempt at achieving height, until 1000
complicated long nave with an attempt at achieving height, 1000
even more complicated long nave with an even greater striving for height, 1130
central structure without height, 1450
compromise of central structure with a long nave, 1540
copies of older styles, 1740
contemporary church architecture 1900 (this type cannot

be summarized in a few words.)
Finally, the sequence of space, the proper element in all
this, is as follows:
simple sacred space, until 1000
doubtful sacred space, from 1000
even more doubtful sacred space, from 1130
failed sacred space, from 1450
forced sacred space, from 1540
copied sacred space, from 1740
new, genuine sacred space, from 1900.

To this sequence I would like to add the year 1959 for
the confirmation of the new sacred space in the announcement of Vatican Council II, which opened in October,
1962. The last two dates constitute a turning point because
this Council meant a revision of the development since 1540.
(The Council of Trent was opened in 1545.) What this
turning point means in terms of church building cannot
be stated yet. For this reason this turning point wasn't
mentioned in the first two sequences. But one can expect
that the consequences will be favorable. There are already
indications to that effect.

Parallel to the sequence of sacred spaces runs a sequence,
equally marked by striking differences, in mysticism which
is the core of religious reality. But we will not consider it
here. And just as clearly parallel with the sequence of sacred
spaces runs a sequence of phases in mathematics and insight or power in the realm of physical science; these
phases also are characterized by striking differences. We
cannot enter into this matter here, for what interests me
at present is the kind of understanding of profane space
which accompanied the phases of development in the scientific picture of the world. And even in this matter I wish

to limit myself here to the following question: what are the phases of man's historically always changing understanding of the shape of the space around the earth?

This much can be said. The conviction that the earth was not flat but round, a sphere, arose in the Christian West for the first time around the year 1000. Initially this conviction was vague and purely theoretical. Between 1450 and 1540 seamen made this spherical shape a concrete reality; they couldn't have done this if the conviction that any place of the earth is as good as any other place had not been a matter of fact for those seamen and their contemporaries, no matter how much some of them at first doubted this. Only on a sphere is every place equal to any other, so that in principle one can travel anywhere.

In 1543 Copernicus published the work in which he defended the conviction that the sun is the center of the universe, not the earth. In 1733, the first study uttering a still restrained non-Euclidean doubt appeared. That was seven years before 1740, the year which, with the addition of "around," marks the end of Baroque and the beginning of the neo-styles. A few years after 1900 the first writing containing the theory of relativity was published. This theory leads to the view that all space is "curved," as it were, a sphere, so that the universe must be finite. This finiteness, this "spherical shape," again leads to the conclusion that any place in the universe can in principle be reached and "walked upon." In 1961, one year before the opening of Vatican Council II, the first man actually went into space.

Briefly put, the sequence is as follows:
a flat earth until 1000
1000, a curved and ever more earth

1450, an earth so curved and so small that all places on it are not only in principle equal but have also become closer, so that seamen and explorers can reach them

1543, a larger and therefore less curved earth in a heliocentric space

1733, non-Euclidean space

1900, curved, finite space

1961, confirmation of this finite space in the launching of the first manned earth satellite.

Much in this series can and must be more closely examined. This will come later, I hope. Besides, the series is not complete. The year 1130, in which the first Gothic churches arose at Saint Denis and Sens, isn't included here. Should any importance be attached to the Crusades in this context? Or is the change of 1130 in the building of churches — a change which I was able to indicate only by the use of comparison — of too little essential importance to be accompanied by a change in man's understanding of the shape of the cosmos? These questions need to be examined more closely, but only the following point interests us here.

If the shape of space, and particularly the shape of the earth is mirrored in the form of man's religious conviction, that is, if the mystical element, the central reality of faith, is mirrored in man's understanding of the shape of the earth and the space around it, and if the style of church building testifies to this reciprocal mirroring, what, then, is *real* in the shape of the earth and of the space around it? We limit ourselves to the first point as to which shape the earth has in reality. Which shape is assigned to it in the most recent period? What was the shape in each period?

Which is truly and really uniquely proper to that period? Was the earth really round before the year 1000 or was it in all reality flat before that time?

Such questions seem unacceptable. But if the earth, before 1000, was not flat in reality, that is, in the reality of the first, underived, most real structure, what right do we have to admit that the earth after 1000 is a sphere? A similar question must be asked at the year 1543, as must also be done for each of the other years in our enumeration. If the earth before 1543 was not in all reality the center of the universe, what right does anyone have to assume that, after 1543, the sun was really that center? Undoubtedly, there are important arguments in favor of the last-named supposition, arguments which seem irrefutable. But all these arguments date from 1543 and later. Many, if not all of them, were evoked by the fundamental insight that the sun is the center, but this insight itself was only barely reasoned, if at all. Would the arguments have been found if that insight had not arisen? Once this insight is given, the arguments, at least the main ones, are readily available.

Moreover, and this is most important, doesn't the comparison of the succeeding periods show that the idea of the sun as the center can only become reality when a crucial insight, borne by many different factors, has been reached, or rather, when a new pattern of life, common to all, has arisen?

The same must be said with respect to the flat earth. When the Romanesque style originated, that is, when the mentality or style of life which led to the building of Romanesque churches, had become consolidated, the spheric shape of the earth found its first, albeit weak, defender. What would have happened if the Romanesque style had not arisen? Everyone would have continued to live with the conviction that the earth is flat; yet in our view, there are many things, even extremely simple things, that plead for the spherical shape. The sun rises and sets, we say; but what would one think of such a statement if one did not know about the earth's spherical shape? Where was the sun between its setting and rising? "Go to the sea shore," says anyone with an elementary education, "and see how first the hull of a ship disappears, then its funnel and finally the plume of smoke." Didn't people see the same in former times while watching sailing vessels, except for the smoke? As a matter of fact, they didn't. And they did not really have any objections to a sun that sets, has gone and then reappears. They were not disturbed by a thing which, in terms of a flat earth, impresses us as an occult kind of acrobatics.

Life evidently was different in those days before the year 1000 – so much different that a flat earth with that kind of a sun above it appeared acceptable. People were just as satisfied with their understanding of the situation as we are with ours. Perhaps they were even more satisfied, for we are not as content now, tired as we are from the constant change in our understanding of the situation. However, *was* the earth flat at that time? How little faith I have! The earth was flat, in the full reality of the first structure of that time. The three series of corresponding eras do not permit any other conviction. But as a child of the twentieth century I am obliged to believe in a spherical earth. I don't even hesitate to generalize my conviction and apply it to all times. But everyone before me in every period has done exactly the same.

Nevertheless, in this twentieth century I have been able to experience bodily how the curvature of the earth has changed in the course of time. This experience evolved with the following facts.

Since the time when the general conviction grew that the earth was spherical — that is, since the year 1000 — there have been many efforts to estimate and, subsequently, to measure, the radius of the earth. At first, these estimates were much too high; next, they were too low. Then they went up again; and finally, through the introduction of the second structure, through measurement, which always leads to constants, a constant length was fixed for the radius of the earth. I asked myself during which period this radius was so underestimated. If my survey was right, it should have been during the period of the Renaissance. As a matter of fact, that radius was underestimated between 1450 and 1540. It was judged to be so small, I figured, that people did not dare to build a church on the curvature of such a small globe, a long church, with an elongated nave, breaking at the apex of the curvature. One doesn't build a long church, I reflected, on a mountain top, unless one can first level this top, and that couldn't be considered with respect to the earth as such. On a mountain top one builds a church with a small foundation, in other words, a circular or polygonal foundation. I realize, of course, that my comparison is deficient. But I cannot get rid of the idea that the conviction of the earth's strong curvature in one way or another prevented the builders of that time from planning and constructing a long church. Later, when the radius of the earth was again estimated to be greater, the Baroque style appeared and re-introduced a long nave.

Let me now discuss the above-mentioned experience. Fortified with the conviction that there is a connection between the spherical shape of the earth and the ground plan of a church, I entered, when next I revisited Rome, the small temple of Bramante, which was finished in 1502 and which has been preserved untouched. On entering it, I could feel the curvature under the soles of my feet! Suggestion, you will say. Of course, I agree, but a suggestion which was effortlessly imposed upon me by this little temple; hence it was not pure suggestion. Next, in the same Eternal City, I entered the Basilica of San Lorenzo outside the walls. My soles remained flat; rather, they became flat, for is it not true that since the year 1000 all of us walk on curved soles? Again, of course, a suggestion is involved here, two even, but again it is not mere suggestion.

Later I visited Chartres. As I beheld the tremendous height of the nave and asked myself what a church is which wishes to deny the earth to such an extent, I felt the earth move under my feet. Another suggestion, no doubt, but a meaningful suggestion which taught me the truth of this earth. In moments such as these I experience with my body that the earth was flat and that later, after the year 1000, it became a globe. First a very large globe; then a very small globe; then again a large globe, and finally a globe with a fixed and constant radius.

The demonstrative or convincing power of such moments, it must be admitted, differs from that of the following modest argument. When Columbus discovered America in 1492, the first globe was made in Europe. This coincidence is meaningful because there is a meaningful connection between that kind of travelling and the spherical shape of the earth. One who does not travel, who does not leave a small, familiar area, has no need for a spherical earth. As far as he is concerned, a spherical earth is strange and unbelievable; it isn't something real, that can immediately be felt. No one believes that the little garden behind his house is spherical or that his home town is shaped that way. At least, I have never noticed it. But the situation changes when I want to travel, especially if I travel by a modern means of transportation. If, for example, I fly to New York, it becomes rather difficult to say that everything below me is entirely flat. Besides, if I wish to be accurate, I have to keep adjusting my watch. The earth is a globe when I travel. But what if I don't travel and don't use an instrument which leads me to the second structure and expresses the nomadic character of modern life? In that case the earth is flat, as flat as a nickel. In the everyday experience one has in his home and garden the earth is not a globe.

I notice nothing of that spherical shape in this garden. The lawn is perfectly level. In the woods, behind the flowers, there are hills. The distance is as high as my eyes, no matter where I am. There is nothing around me that curves. The sun, which will set later, stands above the fields. If the weather stays nice, tomorrow morning I will be able to see the sun from my room, shining over the same earth. I am not worried because I don't know where the sun has been during the night. All there is to it, I know, is that the sun shone over our antipodes. But this doesn't become real to me, as real as the things around me here: the garden, the lawn, the distance, the house.

Here comes my friend. He has kept me waiting a long time.

TIME

"Are you coming?" he calls. In his hands he holds a tray with a bottle, a decanter full of ice water and two glasses. I get up from the grass and stretch, for I have become stiff. The weather is cooler now. A gentle breeze rustles through the leaves of the trees. The sun no longer burns and the sky is full of feathery clouds.

I walk to the house, climb the few steps and sit across from my friend at the table. We talk. The dog stands beside the table, looks at me, wags his tail and barks. Now he would be willing to accept my invitation. As if reading my thoughts, he runs down the steps, across the lawn, looks for the baluster and sniffs it. Then he lies down and takes it in his mouth, biting and chewing it.

"The weather has changed," my friend says, "gee, I really kept you waiting!" We both take a sip. The dog who has gotten up from the lawn with the piece of wood in his mouth, shaking it madly, runs wildly across the grass. My friend watches, surprised. "There goes one of our balusters," he shouts, but I explain that it is the short one. Meanwhile the dog has laid himself down and continues to gnaw the wood. I can imagine that it looks like now; full of tooth marks and covered with saliva.

"What time is it?" my friend asks. From where I am seated I can see the clock inside. It is four o'clock. "Four o'clock," I say, "that is late. Are we going to continue with the job?" He looks at me. "Don't you feel like it?" I really don't feel like it. We have worked all morning, and on the previous days we kept at it without interruption. Besides, I would like to continue my reflections. "Why should we rush?" I argue, "we will finish in time. After all, it is Saturday afternoon." "What an idea!" my friend answers, "the free Saturday afternoon. First a nap, then a stroll to the village, then sitting around a table with cool drinks, and now leisure." But he sighs contentedly and agrees with me.

"Isn't it strange?" he remarks, "now that everyone has the whole Saturday off, the free Saturday afternoon has virtually disappeared. But here, of all things, during our vacation, it has come back. We have again that old feeling of being free." And that is indeed the case. "Let's make ourselves comfortable," I propose. I put the two deck chairs before the open part of the porch, fetch a small table from a room, place it between the two chairs and put the two glasses on it. We sit down. But we are barely seated when my friend gets up again and goes into the house. He returns with a newspaper, sits down again, opens the paper and scans the headlines. "One would forget all about the world here," he says, "would you like a piece?" "Yes," I reply. The section I get contains a picture of a man who hides his face behind his hand. I read that he has been arrested and is accused of mass murder. The names of his alleged victims are unfamiliar to me, but the man himself intrigues me.

He is smartly dressed, and his nicely-shaped hands are carefully manicured. So, these are the hands that did the deed. I read the caption underneath the photograph. "Well, well," says my friend, "now we know that too." He does not care. Why should one become excited over such things? The newspapers make us cynical. Here an act of violence, there so many people starving to death. News from everywhere. In the paper the world is really a globe, a globe of calamities. An advertisement for an airline draws my attention. An enormous plane with the face of a smiling stewardess in the foreground. A mouthful of perfect teeth. The young lady must be happy. I know nothing about her, but she smiles at me as if we have had all kinds of wonderful adventures together.

I raise my knees and put the paper on my legs. It doesn't interest me. Looking over the paper, I can, if I turn my head a little, just look into the room. It is twenty minutes past four. A long second hand moves around the dial. Each time this hand reaches the figure twelve, it stops for a moment as if to deliberate, and then it continues. The hand seems, as it were, quite certain of itself, it is self-willed. It seems to address itself to the figure twelve and say: "You can stay where you are, but time goes on. Good-bye!" Moreover, time goes on, in this way, with this equability and this tempo. No faster, and no slower. Now the hand has reached the twelve again. A moment of pause, I see it, and the minute is gone. The fact has been registered. And then the hand serenely starts a new round.

All the time I spent in reflection, meditating on dimensions, colors, St. Peter's and the shape of the earth, the hand of the clock continued around, thousands of times around. Is that time? I see circles, nothing but circles. A round surface with figures and little lines, over which hands turn round and round. What is time? Here begins my fourth reflection.

Fourth Reflection

When I got up from the lawn and stretched myself, I thought: "It must be late; there is hardly anything left of the afternoon; we won't finish the balustrade today." Next, I wondered why we should rush things; so I made a proposal to my friend, which he accepted. Now we are both lying down in our easy chairs. It no longer seems late now; yet the afternoon is almost gone. It is almost half past four. At half past six we will go to the village for our dinner. That will only be a fifteen minute walk; so we have two hours to wait. Two hours! They were too short to go on with the work, but now they are too long to spend reading the paper. The time from now till dinner has become longer.

The cause of this change lies in our changed intention, our change of plans for the afternoon, which in turn effected a change in time. So it seems. But which time should I view as real? The time in which I intend to go on with the work or that in which I propose that we stop working? What is time without any plan? That would be time without any content. If the content changes, time also changes. I cannot see which content enjoys any preference, for with respect to each and any content time is real.

The first time I looked at the clock this afternoon was when I observed that I had been sitting on the porch for fifteen minutes, that is, one quarter of one hour. An hour is the twenty-fourth part of a day. A day is a unit of time that should be taken seriously. Yet this unit of time reveals, within the limits of its duration, differences that are not negligible. There are days that last forever, and others that fly. The comparison which obviously comes to mind here is that with the measure of length, which I was meditating on early this afternoon. That measure also possesses its own dimension, one which is equally inconstant.

Does this mean that time is connected with the measure of length? If so, I could very easily end up with the circles on the clock. But color also reveals various shades within its own limits. Is there, then, a connection between time and color? Between time and light? In a certain sense there can be no doubt about the latter connection. The twenty-four hour day contains a day and a night; thus it is divided by light. The day time also is divided into morning, noon and evening, which is again a division by light, even by color. But this is not exactly what I am looking for. The question was: when a thing changes color because its place is modified, because I assume a different location with respect to it, or because other things change position in reference to it, does time then occur in the change of color? Did time occur when the clouds grew and all things, through this change, received a new color within the limits of their own color?

I cannot doubt that this should be answered in the affirmative. If the color of things remained constant, time would stop with respect to those things, and no one could know that time flows with respect to them. If the light of the day did not change, that is, if the sun remained in the same place in the sky, no one would still know what time is. Yet the idea still seems strange. Is the progress of time the same as the changing of light and colors? Is the progress of time one and the same with the mutability of dimensions? If the latter were true, then a vertical time would exist side by side with horizontal time. There would be a time of the vertical tower and a time of that tower after its fall. Placed in a vertical position, stones would have a different time. The idea undoubtedly is strange or novel, but is it unacceptable?

When we abandoned the plan to go on with the work, the two remaining hours became longer. But there was more. I said, rather carelessly, that it was Saturday. My friend made that statement much more concrete. When he exclaimed, "the free Saturday afternoon!", he introduced a new change. The Saturday afternoon, which so meaningfully used to be called "free," was characterized by a time of its own; and my friend's exclamation restored the free dimension of the Saturday afternoon. The hours became free, free in a way that isn't the same as that of Sunday's free hours. Originally every day had its own time; and strictly speaking, this is still so today but no longer as clearly as it used to be. Monday, anyhow, still had a color of its own. Together, the days of the week again are different in each season with respect to their colors and lengths.

If I wish, I can note here again for the umpteenth time that "the matter itself" — which is here "the time of the four seasons" — remains the same. But in that case there also arises, again for the umpteenth time, the question as to the criterion by which preference is given to the time of one particular season. What is time without season? It is almost time without time. No one, at any rate, has ever experienced time outside an era, without season, without special colors and dimensions. Surely one cannot say that the road one walks in the winter has the same length as in the summer.

Or should I say that the time of the clock is the genuine time? This is usually done, but it is not convincing. I look into the room. The second hand moves forward over the dial of the clock. Its change in position undoubtedly makes me realize that time goes on. But the realization is more profound and more genuine when I perceive the changes in things. For example, when a thunderstorm is coming, or when I am working, reading a book or hammering at a balustrade. The hand on the clock moves too uniformly to express the time of such moments. The thing that goes round the dial is too abstract and its tempo isn't right. Besides, which tempo should I take? That of the second hand, the minute hand, or the hour hand? These questions are, no doubt, meaningless. While everything that happens has a tempo of its own, the question about the "ownness" of the tempo of the instrument which indicates time is meaningless. Yet this remains strange.

What the three hands have in common is the uniform character of their tempos. Generally speaking, this uniform tempo does not disturb us. Only the second hand becomes irritating after a few rounds. The other two are more easily acceptable. They move so slowly that in a lucky moment one can almost imagine that they stand still. But they do move, and go forward with tedious regularity. Only just a short time ago it was half past five, but now it is one minute later. One minute has gone by. Soon it will be five, then ten, minutes. What is the meaning of such numbers? The day as a unit can be accepted, but what about a fraction of the day? Even half a day, exactly half a day, encounters difficulties.

A morning, afternoon and evening, that is something real. True, there is also a division here, but it is of a different nature. I don't divide the day into parts, but indicate the division which the day itself offers. All I really do is assign names. For this reason I don't worry about the limits. The fact that I don't know exactly where the morning ends and the afternoon begins doesn't trouble me. Yet I do know that no limit will satisfy me. Every day has its own limits for its parts, that is, if one can rightly speak of limits in this context. For what does the limit of time mean? I don't know. A country has its limits or boundaries, and so does a body. But what does it mean to divide time, as such? A body or a surface can be divided, but time? What means or instruments do I have? And once I have an instrument, where am I to place it in time to perform my action of splitting, cutting, sawing or cleaving? Where lies the predesigned section?

On the face of the clock I see three kinds of sections, but with respect to all of them I must say that they are unreal in reference to what is called time. Obviously, I do not deny that an hour is something meaningful. But that which I see and observe as the period "hour," I must locate in a reality if the visible and observed is to have any meaning. For example, an hour of this afternoon has meaning, obviously, but only because the afternoon itself has meaning and because I have learned to divide the afternoon "from twelve o'clock till six o'clock" into six parts. Are six parts or pieces which are not equal adequate terms? The stretch from twelve to one has a different duration compared to that from five to six. The inequality becomes even more evident if I compare the afternoon with the morning. From nine to twelve in the morning is three hours, and from twelve to three in the afternoon is also three hours. But the two periods are far from equal. From nine to twelve in the morning is a long period for some people, and in the winter it is even the entire morning for many; but from twelve to three in the afternoon is hardly more than the beginning of the afternoon. Of course, I shouldn't forget here that the morning, compared with the afternoon, is short in hours. It only has three, four or five hours, while the afternoon has six or seven. But it is precisely this difference that is at issue here. What induces us to divide the morning which is long, longer even than the afternoon, into fewer hours than the afternoon?

"Long," "longer," "short" — I notice that I keep using words borrowed from a spatial order. I even spoke of "period," a "space of time." How, then, can I object to such terms as "parts" or "sections"? It appears impossible to speak of time without using terms that, strictly speaking, apply only to space. Is space that closely related to time? In that case my objections have to be dropped. Let me investigate this point.

A body, a distance or a measure of length can be divided. The baluster was 100 centimeters long, one hundred parts. Although it has become clear to me that the parts are not stable, not even equal, nevertheless, what I am doing in making this division is something real and adequate. I look again at the clock. The time needed for one full circle of the second hand is sixty pieces. Sixty sections struck down by that hand. They are, visibly, sixty pieces of a plane. Or if I refer to the circle painted on the dial, sixty pieces of a line. In other words, what happens there on the dial is a division of planes and lines. Nevertheless, I admit without much opposition the idea that the clock divides time, despite the fact that I see but little of a division of time on the dial. A circular surface, divided into sixty sectors, over which three lines — the hands — perform motions in three tempos; that's all I see.

But those three lines move. And I do not hesitate to speak of tempos. Whatever moves has time, although I must admit at once that the possession of time by the motions which I perceive on the clock is reduced to a minimum by the uniformity of these motions. Yet time remains attached to the clock, undoubtedly because the characteristic of motion has not entirely disappeared from the shifting hands. Time manifests itself in every motion. Any motion is a change, any change is a motion. When colors change, time manifests itself, as it does when dimensions change. When I saw the clouds move in the distance, I saw, most literally, the march of time. When I myself move, time realizes itself just as literally.

From here to the border of flowers is twenty paces, that is, without doubt, twenty pieces of time. From here to the village is a walk of fifteen minutes, again a matter of motion and time. Let me assume that I have to make fifteen hundred paces to reach the village; and let us further assume that my tempo remains the same — an assumption that is dangerous and which will have to be revoked, as we'll see shortly. On these assumptions the time from here to the village is divided into fifteen hundred equal sections. But this statement isn't true. The duration of the paces at the beginning is not equal to that of the paces at the end of my walk. This is true even for the small number of twenty paces from here to the flowers, although in this case it is barely noticeable.

When I marched on my tired feet to Bellinzona the difference was quite clear. The slow, long-lasting paces at the start were of shorter duration than the paces made later on the road. Only close to the end did the paces again take less time. Generally speaking, the duration of paces becomes longer or shorter while one is walking. The length of the steps becomes longer or shorter while one is walking. I have the impression that I am saying the same thing twice. The time of the road changes; the length of the road changes. The two statements are equal. But in that case I may not speak of an equal tempo on my walk from here to the village. If the distances change on that walk — and this is not subject to doubt — then the tempo changes.

What happens now if I assume that the tempo of my walk remains equal, as the clock wishes me to believe is possible? Then the road becomes equally long everywhere. But if a road is everywhere of the same length, it ceases to be a road. A road is a road from here to there. If the road is just as long everywhere, the here and there of that road has been eliminated. By the same token, that which lies between here and there is also eliminated; there is no longer any road. Categorically the road can then no longer be walked on, and categorically time no longer governs the road. Whatever still happens on that road can then be compared with the turning of the hands on the clock. On the clock the dimensions are equal; they have been intentionally made equal. No one should claim that the dimensions could perhaps still be unequal — although they are, for instance, in the difference between horizontal and vertical — for that would spoil the purpose of the clock.

If I accept the clock's purpose, that is, if I call the distances on the dial equal, if, for instance, I deny that the horizontal pieces of the arc at the twelve and the six are unequal to the vertical pieces at the three and the nine, then I deny the distances on the dial. For distance — let me repeat it — is a matter of "from . . . to," with all the differences this implies. But if I deny the distances on the dial, I deny the time of that dial. What it all amounts to is ultimately this: if the aim pursued by the clock would be realized, there would no longer be time. For time is the inequality of dimensions. If the dimensions are equal, then there is no time. If the centimeter here were equal to the (same) centimeter there, there would be no time.

No one, however, has to fear that the clock will realize its aim. The hands go "from ... to," and that is enough, no matter how much the second hand with its conspicuous uniform constancy does its best to conceal this "from ... to," feature. Only at the twelve does the second hand fall short of its role. The moment of waiting disturbs the deliberate equality pursued by the clock, but this moment of waiting should not be taken seriously. It merely means a concession to real, authentic time. There at the twelve, the hand arrives, there it waits a moment, and from there it goes on again. At the twelve the dimensions are different; there a different time rules. Or rather, time rules there, at the twelve when the second hand arrives, stops and departs again. Just as time rules, really rules at the six and the twelve when the clock strikes.

An honest clock doesn't strike; certainly an honest clock doesn't allow the second hand to catch its breath at the twelve. An honest clock is thoroughly complete in its attempt to eliminate time. Once again, however, such an honest clock cannot be realized, not even if the second hand doesn't stop for a moment at the twelve; nor can it be realized if the clock doesn't strike and the familiar figures, which always remind us of arrival and departure, are replaced by neutral short lines of the same kind. The hands go on climbing and descending, and isn't that enough?

Besides, the rate of speed of the hands cannot be undone. The hands do not only go round with a uniform tempo, but this rate of speed has been carefully chosen. This choice isn't essential to the clock's objective. In principle the clock could fulfill its task just as well if the speeds of the hands' movement were smaller or greater. But as far as we perceivers are concerned, the rate of speed assumes some importance. If the clock ran, for example, one hundred times faster, it would be useless for us. Its tempo would be unbelievable and insufficiently adapted to the time we know. On the other hand, a clock running one hundred times slower would make us lethargic. Its tempo, too, would be unbelievable, too little in keeping with the march of time in things and not adapted to their changes in color and dimension.

The clock's tempo has been ingeniously chosen in such a way that neither extremes happen although something does occur. The rate of speed of the hands has been chosen in such a way that the mutability of color and dimension proper to things is hardly affected. The clock thereby shows a caution, close to trickery, which compels admiration. Time as such cannot be measured or registered because time as such is not and cannot be seen. Time as such is not real. What is real is the changing of things, their dimensions and colors. In order to restrain the changing of things, to camouflage this changing as much as possible, the clock was given those tempos which disturb as little as possible.

If the clock went faster, we would say: no color or dimension changes with such a speed. If it went slower, we would say: nothing around us changes so slowly. The changing of things, of their colors and dimensions, would draw attention. But the speed that has actually been given to the clock peacefully harmonizes with the speed at which things change — so peacefully that this change draws as little attention as possible and people are induced to think that this changing in color and dimension isn't true, doesn't even happen. This goal has been marvellously reached.

There is hardly anybody who still thinks that things change in reality.

It would be wrong, however, to think that the clock as an instrument is the cause of all this. The clock is an invention, and it is in the mentality which led to this invention where the true cause must be sought. When was the clock invented, that is, in its modern form with a first attempt to be precise? The question cannot be easily answered. If I had to make a guess, I would say: at the time when the earth became a sphere, that is between 1000 and 1450. What is certain is that in the first half of the fourteenth century the first mechanical clocks were installed on the towers of the city halls in the most important European cities. The oldest description of a mechanical clock dates from the decade of 1370. Who invented this kind of clock, and when, is not known, but it isn't likely that it happened long before the first description.

This would mean that the first development of what later was to become a precision instrument lies in the last phase of high Gothic, the era in which the earth began to become a sphere for many people. Why this connection? The spherical surface is the one which least of all surfaces gives the impression of distance. On a sphere all points are in principle equal. On a pure sphere no one can travel; at most, one can relocate himself there in the way the hands of a clock go round. On the basis of this connection it is to be expected that the history of the earth's spherical shape and that of the circular motion of the hands on a clock will be chronologically related.

A general need for an *accurate* division of time arose in the eighteenth century. I could assume that it has arisen since 1740, that is, since the end of Baroque style, the end of sacred space, authentic for the period, or since the beginning of space that is uniform and identical everywhere. Before that time, most people were satisfied with a day consisting of two parts, the part of the rising sun and that of the setting sun. The need to move faster over the earth also arose in the eighteenth century. The light-weight stage-coach made its appearance, the horses were changed more frequently, so that a trip could be even quicker. The same century saw the invention and use of the precursor of the modern telegraph.

In harmony with these new needs and the new ways of doing things arising from them, the desire to deny the changing of things became prevalent in that century. The idea of evolution was born, and it held that everything our eyes see, whether living or non-living, originated through inner necessity from raw, timeless matter, so that every-thing is and remains essentially the same as that matter. At the same time there arose ideas which later developed into the psychological theory of projection, a theory which implies that the changes in color and dimension can be unmasked as merely apparent so far as reality is concerned. Since then change occurs in us as an idea or a suggestion, but the things themselves remain the same.

Our century, however, the twentieth century, possesses again a sacred space of its own, as is manifest in the style of church building of the past few decades. And in this century this proclaimed unity of events is under attack. The theory of evolution leaves room for the idea of muta-tion — conceived in the year 1901 — in which the principle of graduality is given up and the theory defended that really new, really unequal, beings can arise with a leap from existing forms of life through the working of hitherto obscure factors. In physical science also since 1900 progress is made by the idea that not only gradual events but also events which occur abruptly underlie the properties and changes of matter. Moreover, a few years before 1900 physical science saw the revolutionary hypothesis that the dimensions of objects depend on their motion. Virtually unacceptable at that time, this hypothesis received new significance a few years after 1900 in the theory of relativity; it was then flanked by the no less revolutionary view, now generally accepted, that time — concretely, the time needed by the hands of the clock to go round — depends on the motion of the system in which the observer is situated.

These few summary and general remarks need, of course, to be expanded. But the only point at stake here is this: in the period from about 1740 till 1900, the period of neo-styles and the corresponding uniformity of space on earth, the stability of things was held to be beyond dispute, while before 1740 the conviction of stability had not been dominant. After 1900 it has again been given up. That is, it has been given up in various sciences, but hardly as yet outside the sciences. One could not possibly maintain that since 1900 people have generally abandoned the postulate of the stability of things. Be this as it may, in the period 1740-1900 the duration of things was overestimated at the expense of their tempo.

Duration and tempo — this was the theme of my reflection in Chapter Two. I concluded there that things possess time, they have duration and tempo. Time as duration is the identity of things, the consistency of their color and dimension. To this we must now add that the *duration* of things tempts us to assume that they do not change but remain the same. The world then becomes dry and nameless; ultimately even nothing but a formula. The tempo of things can induce us to believe in a "lawless," arbitrary, even enchanted world. Both these extremes must be rejected. Things not only have duration but also tempo.

In the period 1740-1900 duration was overestimated. That wouldn't have been possible if things hadn't presented themselves as having much duration and little tempo. Things with more duration than tempo impress us as dead or dying. It is no coincidence that in the period 1740-1900 the idea arose that through the irreversible process of cooling, the world as a whole faces *death by cooling,* or, in official terms, *heat death.* Between 1740 and 1900 things were already more or less dead. At any rate, they had lost their luster, which is seen in the fact that the era was characterized by its inclination to strip things of anything that would inspire wonder. One who denies the wondrous aspect of things — that is, their changeability — loses respect for them. Once this respect has suffered, one can handle things casually. One handles them in this way when one passes them quickly. He who moves with speed through a landscape proves that he has little respect for the things in it. Thus, the increasing velocity of locomotion in the period 1740-1900 can be seen as an expression of the overestimation for the duration of things that prevailed at that time.

It is obvious that the speed of locomotion has not decreased since 1900. On the other hand, it is just as true that the glorification of the duration of things has disappeared. Only in certain sciences views are proposed which favor their mutability, and even there these views are often concealed in complex arguments which, moreover, are always accompanied by an objectivistic explanation related to the duration of things. What would happen if the mutability of things again gained the upperhand? We would then abandon the means of fast transportation, a thing which at present we could scarcely imagine.

Yet, this expectation cannot simply be rejected. In order to see things change one has to stop his car. Experience shows this. But perhaps I should rather fear that the present and future velocity of locomotion will gain the upperhand over the tempo of things which has just now again become perceptible, so that the duration of things will again prevail. Or is perhaps a compromise possible, in the sense that rapid locomotion will increasingly occur only at a very high altitude or below the ground, thereby becoming invisible — as is already the case with modern jet planes — so that locomotion on the surface of the earth can again become slow? Time will tell.

But why talk about the future? The future has always been different than one could have expected on the basis of the data given in the past and the present. Let me rather return to the task at hand, reflection on the tempo of things, not their duration. This kind of reflection is appropriate to my time, the twentieth century.

Tempo, I said is the changing of dimensions and colors. This definition is onesidely visual, especially if I were to put the accent on colors; it could lead one to suspect that a blind man perceives less time and, in particular, less tempo. It is true, no doubt, that a blind man perceives time differently and therefore also lives differently; nevertheless, even the blind man has perceptions, so that he, just as well as the others, experiences time and in equal measure. What he lacks in the perception of things by his inability to see colors and dimensions, he compensates for in his auditory and tactile perception of sounds and shapes, in which he surpasses those who can see. One who can see is, as a rule, too visually orientated to appreciate in a proper way the tempo, as well as the duration, of things that can be perceived with the other senses. This concept assures me that the following reflection can be followed by the blind man, who has taught me so much about perception.

Let me recall my hike to Bellinzona. In my imagination I see the long, straight road before me. It seemed endless. That wasn't really the case, of course, for I could see the town in the distance and, as a matter of fact, I really did arrive there. Yet the road was long, so long that the one hundred meter markers made a very strange impression on me. Besides, the distances between those markers weren't the same. Those in the middle were longest; thereafter, they became shorter again; and the last distance was so short that I don't even recall walking it.

At that time on that road I perceived time. The one hundred meter markers served as my measuring rod in that perception — I kept looking at them — but not because I could believe that the markers indicate the true lengths of the stretches of road. In that respect the markers are misleading. The road had become longer, much longer, before my eyes, just as the distances on the road had become longer. I didn't have to see the markers. The measuring rod provided by them was a measuring rod for people who are tired, that is, for my equals-without-time, for timeless beings. I saw the duration of the road in those markers, and this reinforced my perception of the road's tempo. That's why I looked at those markers.

Later when I went the same way by car I hardly looked at the markers. The road was sheer duration, which made the markers, those proofs of duration on the road, inconspicuous. What struck me was that the poverty of the road; it has become unrecognizable. I had expected a more striking impression, a more convincing distance, more convincing mountains. Nevertheless, it was the same road, with the difference that it possessed less tempo and more duration. In accordance with this, the distances between the markers was equal, at least more or less equal. I suspect that the distances would have been entirely equal if I had been able to roar over the road in an airplane; I am even convinced that, in a manner of speaking, the distances would have been equal within one thousandth of a millimeter if I had been able to move over them with the speed of light. The road would then have frozen into sheer duration, so that no time whatsoever would have been present on it.

For time, taken now as encompassing both duration and tempo, is realized only in the changing, no matter how small, of dimensions and colors. Time exists only when one "takes the time," both duration and tempo. Time is realized while one strolls through a city. Time becomes concrete while one climbs a mountain top or a tower. The verbs "strolling" and "climbing" are important here. One who strolls through a city, in and out of streets and lanes, stopping and passing on, actually goes from one time to another. Each street has a different time, provided one respects the verbs appropriate to that street. The Quartier Latin of Paris has a different time than the suburbs of Passy or Auteuil. One's watch is either fast or slow, depending on the street.

In some cities certain quarters are governed by a time, so unique to them, that one is greatly surprised by it. Such a surprise can, for instance be found when one leaves the teeming streets around the Piazza Navona in Rome and enters this square. Sitting down on the edge of one of the three fountains, one can then find the other verbs appropriate to this Piazza. A similar surprise but on a smaller scale, which makes it perhaps all the more convincing, is experienced when one sees and enters one of the small cool inner courtyards of a house in southern Spain: a *patio andaluz,* with its tiny dripping fountain, its flowers and subdued light, and its unique time, which hardly makes any progress.

It isn't necessary, however, to travel very far; this difference of time can be experienced within the confines of a small section of a single city. At the Grand Central Station of New York time flows faster than in Central Park. Must I, because of this, fear being late for the train if I walk from the Park to the Station? That is indeed possible, if I take the Park's time and the verb "to walk" which accompanies it with me to the Station. Usually, however, I leave the verb and the time in the Park when I hurry to the Station. Each place, through its proper tempo, invites me to its own kind of going, walking, hurrying, as well as seeing and hearing. But this doesn't mean that one may not "sin" against that proper kind of going and perceiving of that place, either out of necessity or for the sheer delight of it.

Each place has its own time. The examples I have seen this afternoon have convinced me of that. The most striking of them was the following. While everything around me was motionless and time was almost at a standstill in the massive heat of the day, the distant masses of clouds were turbulent. The vague contours of these clouds were full of motion. Yet the clouds didn't become visibly larger, and the motions of the cloud formation which I was watching were barely perceptible. There was more motion, I think, in the minute hand of the clock than in what I saw there.

I didn't make the comparison at that time but don't

think that this is necessary to see that the comparison isn't adequate. What I saw there was a giant movement but no separate motions. On the clock I would see just the opposite: moving hands and hardly any movement. The clouds had tempo but little duration. The clock has duration and hardly any tempo. The clouds had time. The clock is full of rest. Let us leave the clock alone and remember the masses of turbulent clouds with their separate, tense parts at a standstill. Time moved faster in those parts, faster than the time between the trees, faster than the time on this porch. There were different times in that one panorama. Times, differing in speed, existed together in one and the same landscape.

Is it possible, then, for times which differ in tempo to be united in a single landscape? I have actually seen it effortlessly, and I still see it now although the differences are smaller now. In between the flowers a different time prevails than on the lawn. Time goes a little faster there. Above me, among the feather clouds, time goes even faster. Nothing proves that this isn't possible. An effortless unity governs what I see, a unity in time, strange as it may seem. For just now when I observed for the first time that in different places time moves at a different speed, I thought that I therefore ought to conclude that the places of such different times couldn't possibly remain synchronous. One place would lag behind the others and be stuck with a surplus of time at the end of the day, while other places would run short. But I see my mistake: I was fooled by the idea of an absolute, uniform, uniformly progressing time possessing only one speed. I must abandon that idea. I don't know what I am supposed to do with that idea of an absolute time having only one speed either. Which speed? Even the hands on the clock have three different speeds, and these don't interfere with one another. Why, then, should I worry about the different times revealed by a single landscape?

There are numerous examples of different times, connected with certain simple data. The sea has a different time than the land. A lake in a forest is a realm of a different time. Sometimes a single tree or bush can draw attention because of the distinctive time prevailing around it. There are flowers which disclose new times at certain moments of the day. When the thorn-apple opens up in the evening, a new and faster time governs this flower. And the real reason isn't that the flower moves at that time, but just the opposite. Because a different time governs that flower in the evening, the flower opens quickly in that particular way and invites the hawk-moth, which is endowed with fast time and flies precisely in that particular way. For what is speed if it isn't born by speedy, "time-consuming" things, plants or animals?

Compared with the toad, the frog is fast, even when it doesn't stir and, on the basis of its particular speed, the frog leaps, while the toad crawls by virtue of the time that is its own. Even people have a time of their own; each one, I suspect, has one for himself. The botanist is marked by a different time than the geologist. The zoologist who specializes in diptera is by virtue of his time, his tempo and duration, a different man than his colleague who prefers to limit himself to bumble bees. Compare the gracefully and rapidly alighting dragonfly with the busy, ungainly, searching bumble bee: they represent two tempos, two forms of time, and the zoologist has to make a choice if he wishes to have the specific interest which he professes to have.

In this way everyone has his own specific time. The length of the day varies for each one. If this length differs for two persons, their relationship can be adversely affected by it. It isn't likely that a marriage will last if the times of man and wife are too divergent. Two different tempos permanently at the same table, not to mention the same bed. One doesn't plant two flowers close together in the same plot if they differ very much in their use of time. The one would ruin the other's time. Or am I exaggerating? Is my imagination running wild?

I am quite capable, of course, of imagining things. Just as I can become guilty of illusions, so also can I let myself be carried away on the wings of fancy. I am capable of letting my thoughts run wild, I can cling to a shadow, try to seize a chimera. I have tried not to let this happen. But now, in what follows, why should I not do it for once, out here on the porch? Let us go then.

The moment is appropriate. The sky is again assuming colors. The scenery is grand and is becoming more and more mysterious through the change in weather and the approaching sunset. The woods to the right seem less penetrable. Can I enter the woods and boldly walk around in them? Of course, I can, but right now, I don't wish to do it. I let the dusk in the woods become strong and powerful, so that it keeps me out of them. Imagination is captivating me. The woods have become less accessible in a way and with a speed suggesting that they have found their own character in that inaccessibility.

Fancy? The reality which I perceive is real enough. Without effort, more or less even against my inclination at first, but rapidly more and more with my consent, I now discover this reality which rejects and blocks me also in other places. Out there among the flowers. The border, that flaming mass of luxuriant plants, becomes slightly hostile. Then other things happen. Even the meadow, which has been nothing but a trivial piece of land all afternoon is now a field of suspicion. As long as I retain this impression, I could be made to enter it only by force. The scenery is alien, ominous, hardly accessible, full of places that are blocking me in ever-different ways. How could I ever walk freely around in it? What kind of carelessness held me in its power when I thoughtlessly overcame the barriers? For what I see now is a realm of separate places, each one containing its own terror. Is there still a piece of safe ground? The menace increases, it overpowers me. Oh, beloved, familiar, hostile, terrifying world! Leave me my porch, my chair, my small free space.

That was a phantasy. There is nothing, I just let my imagination run wild. Right, that was all. But what possessed me to do this? I am able to repeat this fancy at once. All I have to do is look at the scenery with a certain expectation and take a certain aspect of it seriously. So, I must ask myself: what am I doing when I walk around on the earth in my daily life? Do I rightly view my world as not having barriers or have I been carefully trained to deny barriers? Am I free or only careless? Is the world I know uniform, everywhere, or different in many places and therefore multiform and not the same everywhere? Is the space around me full, equally occupied by points everywhere? Or is that space not full but broken, open, discontinuous? Does the world have pores, splits, holes? I wouldn't dare to answer in the negative.

The baluster, which has so often played a role in my reflections this afternoon, lies abandoned on the lawn. The grass there has a purplish tone and abruptly comes to an end near the gnawed wood. I can vaguely see something of the tooth marks which the dog has left on it. One side of it is splintered. Saliva glistens in the sun. The dog left something living on the wood; the latter itself has assumed a beastly feature, it is nasty and disgusting. I wouldn't like to put my hand all around it. I can also calmly admit that there is a barrier between that piece of wood and the grass. The grass ends at that barrier; I can see that, even study it. There is a fissure, a gap, a strip of nothingness between the grass and the wood, a little strip where time stands still.

I remember a walk I took in the gardens of Versailles. It was a marvellous springday and I had all the time in the world. I strolled wherever a place looked attractive without paying any attention to orientation. I must have been deep in thought, for suddenly I stood before a hedge which I hadn't even noticed when approaching it. A beech hedge, just too high to look over it. There was a passage to my right, near a small greenhouse. I went to it, passed through the open gate and to my delighted surprise found myself in an enclosed garden full of *azalea mollis*. A garden of yellow and pink hues, drenched by the light of the most delightful spring sun. It was warmer in the garden than out beyond the hedge. I stopped, was tempted to penetrate deeper into the garden, but I didn't do it, for it seemed to me that I didn't have the right to do it.

That's what I recall of that moment. But the peculiar aspect of my experience was this that later I was unable to find that garden again. I earnestly looked for it many times, but always in vain. The last time I looked, I was almost afraid that I might find it. Wasn't that garden more beautiful, more delightful and more genuine now that I couldn't find it? By finding it again, I would have made it less beautiful, less genuine, less familiar. My own mysterious garden of Versailles. So, I stopped looking. That was the kind of garden it was, not to be found.

Was the garden really not to be found? It would have been possible to find it if I had consulted a map of the Versailles park and scrutinized all its little squares. I would then certainly have been disappointed by what I found. Perhaps a small doubt would have remained whether the garden I had seen, so full of light and colors, so full of wondrous surprises, was really the garden which I had found again, an ordinary garden, located by consulting a map of the Versailles park. With a map it isn't difficult to disturb the reality of the most delightful memory. Or should I say that the map shuts off *nothingness* around the special, closed, shut-off reality that can only be experienced in privileged moments? Should I say that the map would have ruined that precious time of my garden?

I have another similar memory which I cannot forget. As a boy of about ten, I once went looking for plants near my hometown. The region was familiar to me. But what happens when one is young and enjoys the privilege of roaming through an old landscape that has not yet been subdivided into small lots? One discovers new spots all the time. While looking for plants and not expecting anything special, I approached a small village. A few houses stood together there without any semblance of order. I had often seen the village but never those houses. One of them was a tavern, as was indicated by a sign with large letters. The door as well as the window above it stood open. It was around noon and perfectly still. I looked at the tavern and the open door, showing the presence of human beings, but no one was visible.

All of a sudden the noise of a mechanical organ poured out through the door. It was terrible. The tempo, the vigor, the vulgar melody, the violence of sound tore the noonday to pieces. I found it both horrible and delightful. When the tune was finished, everything was even more quiet than before. I was hoping for a repeat, but nothing happened. The tune kept resounding in my ears for a whole week. "Saturday," I told myself, "I'll go back." But I was disappointed. No matter how carefully I searched, I couldn't find those six houses and that tavern. I tried several other times, but always in vain, before I finally gave up. But the melody stayed with me and often reminded me of that afternoon. Those six houses, the tavern with its open door, the quiet, and then the infernal noise that tore the quiet to pieces.

Years later, on a bicycle trip, I suddenly stood before those six houses. That was the place! In a strange way I felt caught and, somewhat amusingly, ashamed. How trivial all of it was. Six wretchedly constructed houses and a dilapidated tavern. Was that all? Of course, it wasn't all. My boyhood had passed, I was cycling, I had plans, I no longer searched haphazardly, I no longer roamed around. At least no longer as I used to do, without any orientation. I knew the roads and was familiar with distances. The region which had become a map, wasn't one yet when I first sought plants there. I had shut it off. I had let the duration of the region prevail over its tempo. This made it possible to find that spot again when I was no longer looking for it. Perhaps, if I had sought with the old intention, the six houses and the tavern would have remained unfound and thus untouched. One who follows a map finds everything. Or does he find very little if anything at all? One who wishes to find must roam around, he must even be subject to getting lost. He must be able to ask himself; where am I?

That's what I have done this afternoon, this Saturday afternoon on and in front of the porch of my friend's summer home. I lost myself in thought, wandered around and got lost in the scenery before me, in the garden, the flower border, the woods, the meadow and the distance. My eyes wandered over the facade of this house and I recalled other facades which, unbound by time, I had learned to appreciate, despise and admire. And the things I have found!

I have found that the dimensions of things change, become larger or smaller, according to rules that can immediately be known. I have found that colors play their own game, and that this game also is governed by rules which are meaningful and show that order prevails in the things around us. I have found that the facts and regularities of "the second structure," which, taken separately, should be called accidental and which prohibit the use of the term "meaning," together are needed for the attainment of this one goal that the earth is inhabitable. I have found that there is a connection between such divergent matters as physical sciences and faith, so that time is a possession of things, that things have duration and tempo, and have it in different measures, so that they differ locally and their places also are different. I have found that the world isn't uniform. I have found, I have found . . .

But I have found very little compared to all that can be found. I have found a few small crumbs of all the splendor in which we live.

Allow me the right not to have to rediscover what I have found, by means of a map, that is, only as duration. It would disappoint me. I would not be able to believe in it. But I want to believe in it. Isn't it my duty to preserve what I have found? What I have found makes me live and one day will enable me to die. The nature of a landscape without tempo, the landscape of "between 1740 and 1900," has a death of its own, death by cooling, its "heat death." So be it. The nature of this afternoon this twentieth century afternoon, is my possession, a gift which I wish to preserve intact and which, when my time comes, I wish to surrender intact.